Generis
PUBLISHING

Legislative Interest In Consumers Rights And Its Applications Within Modern Legislations

SAMI BENHAMLA

Title: **Legislative Interest In Consumers Rights And Its Applications Within Modern Legislations**

ISBN: 979-8-89248-736-8

Author: SAMI BENHAMLA

Cover image: https://pixabay.com/ru/

Publisher: Generis Publishing
Online orders: www.generis-publishing.com
Contact email: info@generis-publishing.com

TABLE OF CONTENTS

List of abbreviations

ADR	Alternative Dispute Resolution
ODR	Online Dispute Resolution
ANSES (NAFEOHS)	National Agency for Food, Environmental and Occupational Health Safety
CPL	Consumer Protection Act
CRA	Consumer Rights Act
EC	European Commission
ECOSOC	United Nations Economic and Social Council
ESCWA	United Nations Economic and Social Commission for Western Asia
EU	European Union
FDA	Food and Drug Administration
GDPR	General Data Protection Regulation
GLDC	General Law for the Defence of Consumers
ICA	Italian Competition Authority
LGPS	Decree on General Product Safety
LUC	Law on Unfair Competition
RDL	Royal Decree-Law
ROCU	International Organization of Consumer Unions
UAE	United Arab Emirates
UK	United Kingdom
UNGCP	United Nations guidelines for consumer protection
UUPK	Undang-undang Perlindungan Konsumen

Preface

Requested by my colleague Professor Sami BENHAMLA, to preface his new book, I could only accede to this request; it is an honor for me first and foremost, to be chosen among other colleagues more familiar with the issue, it is also a duty towards a colleague with whom I have exchanged a lot in the field of legal sciences, particularly during international conferences, and finally it is a responsibility towards the readership to whom we owe all our loyalty.

"**Legislative interest in consumers rights and its applications within modern legislations**", is the title of the book, very revealing of the novelty of the subject and its topicality as well as the originality of its methodology.

Consumer rights are not only the concern of lawyers, but also interest economists; politicians, and others alike. This is a new generation of rights that is shaking up all countries in the world nationally, regionally and internationally; and hence the diversity and proliferation of legislation, as well as international legislation. Recently, this new generation of rights has taken into account its specifics - particular concepts and new approaches in accordance with the new social, economic and political realities - impacts on the law that can be described as classic. These are the main aspects of this work.

The author tried to highlight this proposition in the book according to a modern methodological approach that combines the historical development of the emergence of consumer rights, which was the cradle of the United States of America, and its development within European countries and the rest of the world, which gave consumer rights a global character in parallel with the efforts of the United Nations that strengthened the emergence of international interest in them, and their recognition within the categories of basic rights, despite the jurisprudential controversy surrounding this topic, on the one hand.

On the other hand, establishing the idea of interest to consumers' rights, as Islamic law is considered the first to pay attention to consumers' contractual rights, especially the right of withdrawal, which legislation recently adopted within the framework of distance contracting.

The author has well addressed the content of consumers rights and their correlation to competition law, which makes promoting these rights one of its most important goals.

He also gave the book a modern character when it addressed consumer rights related to digital contracting as an area related to protecting consumer privacy and a modern field that requires more research. It also highlighted the role of consumer protection associations in defending consumer rights, especially the judiciary type, in light of the legal recognition of its representation on behalf of consumers.

Ali Filali

Professor of Civil Law

University of Algiers1

Bin Youssef bin Khadda

Introduction

Interest in the topic of consumer rights has become a focus of interest for economists and politicians, in addition to jurists. This is what the USA knew at the beginning of the second half of the last century, it was credited with laying the first foundations for consumer's rights, because of growing awareness about the necessity of paying attention to the category of consumers, as they constitute the axis that Market economy policies are based on. Although Islamic law was one of the first laws to pay attention to the rights of consumers, this was particularly clear in the rights related to contracting[1].

In this context, modern legal systems have witnessed several developments thanks to the development witnessed by modern economic life because of the openness of markets to free competition and the consecration of economic freedoms, which led to the expansion of the scope of contractual freedom and contracts of consummation. This situation affected the legal positions of consumers in the market and their interests economic. As the weakest party in the contractual relationship and the important link in the wheel of the market economy, legislators intervened to establish legal protection for consumer rights, which led to the emergence of consumer protection legislation, and before that, constitutional principles enshrining a new generation of basic rights. Which led to the emergence of a protectionist economic public order, that takes into account social issues in contractual and economic relations, which led to a change in the role of the state and the role of the legal rule, which became aimed at achieving protectionist goals more than they are general and abstract.

International interest in the topic of consumer rights has also emerged at the level of the United Nations, where interest in consumers rights has become one of the greatest concerns of governments, states and organizations in the world thanks to the growing legal awareness among the consumer group as well as the interest of economists and politicians in the necessity of establishing and protecting consumers rights. Which led to a widening scope of interest in it, especially in Europe, Asia, and the rest of the world, including the Arab countries, especially Algeria. Which tried to keep pace with this new trend, in a way that enhances the protection of consumer rights

---

[1] Sami Benhamla, Legislative Attention in Consumers' Rights, a New Approach within Modern Legislations: Qatari and Algerian Legislations as Models, International Review of Law, Qatar University Press, vol 13, n01, 2024, p47.

as a new category of basic rights, which resulted from the developments witnessed in modern economic life and the market economy.

Thanks to the contributions of jurisprudence, the judiciary, and the struggle of consumer protection associations and politicians, the idea of consumer rights was established within modern constitutions and consumer protection legislation, which led to the recognition of consumer rights within modern legal systems. In addition to competition law, which has contributed significantly to the promotion of consumers rights by improving the consumer welfare, given that the latter constitutes one of the goals of competition law, as long as the consumer group represents a pivotal group in the market economy.

The protective aspects of consumers rights have also multiplied to include contractual protection of the consumer, the rights related to which constitute one of the most important foundations of consumer rights that have been recently included in legislation, because of their importance in protecting the interests of consumers.

Therefore, the legislator intervened to enshrine contractual rights for consumers within these relationships in order to achieve contractual balance, which made the contractual relationships concluded between the Companies and the consumer characterized by contractual imbalance, in addition to the abusive character that may result from this. Thanks to the attractive advertisements placed by major international companies in order to attract the largest possible audience, which influence consumers' decisions thanks to sales techniques that affect their behavior due to temptations and promotional policies, as well as the culture of freeness that has been known in the digital services of the giants of the digital economy, led by GAFAMs.

In this context, Islamic law, with its principles and provisions, is considered the first to address the topic of protecting consumer rights, and this is what appears through the jurisprudence of sales and its provisions, which established the rules on which recent consumer protection legislation has been based, and this is especially evident in the visibility option that established the emergence of The right to withdraw within the framework of electronic and digital contractual relations conducted remotely.

Besides, the issue of privacy protection emerges, which aims to protect consumer data of a personal nature within the framework of electronic and digital contracting, which resulted in the emergence of protective rules within the framework of adopting a protective public economic system that was linked to protecting the weak party in contractual relations within the framework of the new economic pattern that resulted from Digital transformation.

Consumer protection associations also played a major role in defending and protecting consumers' rights at the judicial level, and this led to the emergence of a mechanism for collective lawsuits to defend the economic and moral interests of consumers, which was considered one of the most important modern requirements for protecting consumers' rights.

These issues and their details will be studied according to the following plan:

Section 1: The emergence of the idea of concerning consumers rights and its development in the world

Chapter 1: The emergence of the idea of interest in consumer rights in the USA and the beginning of international interest in them

Chapter 2: Development of interest in consumers rights in European laws and some countries in the world

Section 2: **The content of consumer rights and the role of competition law in promoting them**

Chapter 1: Consumer rights content

Chapter 2: The role of competition law in promoting consumers rights

Section 3: Protective aspects of consumers rights

Chapter 1: Promoting consumer rights in contractual relationships

Chapter 2: Establishing consumer rights in the digital space when processing data of a personal nature

Chapter 3: The role of consumer protection associations in defending consumers rights

Section 1.

The emergence of the idea of concerning consumers rights and its development in the world

The idea of interest in consumer rights emerged in the United States of America because of the growing political awareness of the necessity of establishing and protecting consumer rights, as they are the category on which the market economy is based.

This had a positive impact on the emergence of international interest at the level of the United Nations and the expansion of the movement of interest in consumer rights across most countries in the world, especially in Europe.

Chapter 1.

The emergence of the idea of interest in consumer rights in the USA and the beginning of international interest in them

The idea of interest in consumer rights began to emerge thanks to politicians who contributed greatly to highlighting this interest because the consumer class constitutes a group that requires preserving its rights in light of the market economy that the economies of the United States of America, especially after World War II (**I**).

If the United States of America is credited with highlighting interest in consumer rights, this contributed greatly to talking about the beginning of international interest in consumer rights at the level of the United Nations since 1985(**II**).

1. The emergence of the idea of interest in consumer rights in the United States of America

Since the end of the nineteenth century and the beginning of the twentieth century, the United States of America has sought to pay attention to consumer rights and establish legislative protection for this category. This was evident in the Wiley Food and Drug Act of 1906, which prohibited dishonest labeling and manufacturing in food sales. This law was considered an introduction to the Federal Food, Drug, and Cosmetic Law in the United States [2].

In addition, the American legislature enacted the Sherman Antitrust Act of 1890[3] . These attempts constitute a prelude to the beginning of a new movement to pay

---

[2] Food law in the United States of America is a body of laws and regulations governing food production, distribution, and consumption that aims to protect consumers. Food lawyers focus their careers on helping producers comply with food laws and regulations. Contributing to the development and implementation of food laws and policies.

There are federal, state, and local food laws. Federal government passes laws such as the Food and Drug Administration Revitalization Act Through the Food and Drug Administration (FDA), the federal government establishes additional regulations and takes steps to enforce federal food law. There are also extensive state laws that typically govern topics such as packaging, distribution, adulteration, and fraud in the food industry.

See, https://www.ksalim.com/2022/07/food-law.html

Accessed: 24/09/2024.

[3] Christian Bolze, "Society, Consumption", Legal Encyclopedia, (1996): 2.

attention to the category of consumers in light of the liberal economy adopted by the United States of America. This topic has also known great political interest since 1962, and this was evident in the speech of US President John Kennedy on March 15, 1962 before the US Congress (Senate), and the House of Representatives (elected house of representatives) when he opened his speech with expressions about protecting consumer interests: "The concept of the consumer includes all of us, and consumers are the largest economic group in the economy that is affected and influenced by public and private economic decisions, and tripartite spending is based on the consumer. And consumers are the most important group in the economy, but they are a group that is not organized as well, their opinion is not heard".

This speech had a positive impact on interest in consumer rights in the United States of America and other industrialized countries, especially in Europe, and March 15, 1983 became World Consumer Protection Day, although this movement experienced several interruptions and periods of stagnation[4].

Between 1969 and 1976, the United States Congress drafted the most important laws concerning the protection of consumer rights [5]:

- The Clean Air Act Amendments Act of 1970
- The Egg Products Inspection Act of 1970
- The Poison Prevention Packaging Act of 1970
- The Consumer Product Safety Act of 1972
- The Agricultural and Consumer Protection Act of 1973
- The Consumer Product Warranties Act - Improvement to the FTL Act of 1974
- The Privacy Act of 1974
- he Equal Credit Opportunity Act of 1975
- The Consumer Leasing Act of 1976.

Besides! the ability of champions of the consumerist cause to put pressure on politicians with a view to obtaining new legislative and regulatory initiatives. Organized consumer groups also played an important role[6].

---

[4] Nicolas Mathey, "Should we Defend Consumer Law", Review Contracts Competition Consumption (2016): 1.

[5] Bryner Gary C, "Consumer protection in the United States: Birth and decline of the regulatory approach", French journal of public administration, N°56 (1990) :592-594.
See, https://www.persee.fr/doc/rfap_0152-7401_1990_num_56_1_2402;
Accessed; 24/09/2024.

[6] Bryner Gary, op cit, p 596.

Mr. Nader himself launched a "flotilla" of groups, from the Center for Science in the Public Interest to multiple Public Interest Research Groups. These groups provided analysis of company practices and agency inadequacies that were critical to justifying new legislative actions. Therefore, the Consumer Federation of America led by Carol Foreman, a loose coalition of groups formed in 1968, demonstrated the extent of support for consumer protection. While the consumers' union, an organization which, for a long time. Dedicated itself to comparative testing and the dissemination of information on the safety and suitability of the goods sold to fulfill their function, adopted a stronger public profile and openly fought for more texts that are aggressive[7].

The birth of the consumer rights movement in the United States of America had a major impact on the emergence of interest in consumer rights in the rest of the world, especially Canada[8].

I. International interest in consumer rights

The movement of interest in consumer rights expanded at the international level, as the United Nations adopted the Global Charter on Consumer Rights en 1985 (**1**), and within this framework, jurisprudence examined the issue of the place that consumer rights occupy within the human rights system and this had a positive impact in enacting many Legislation protecting consumer rights. Thus, this shift constituted the beginning of discussions about a new generation of human rights at the time it adopted Many countries around the world protect consumer rights (**2**).

1- The efforts of the United Nations to establish consumer rights:

The United Nations guidelines for consumer protection (UNGCP) constitutes another step in the international recognition of consumer rights as human rights.

---

[7] Ibid, p 596.

[8] In Quebec: Under the influence of the movement of interest in consumer rights in the United States of America, the Quebec legislature promulgated a consumer protection law in 1971. Revised in 1978, Quebec's Consumer Protection Act (CPL) was born from the social desire to establish rules to protect the interests of the consumer. This law would therefore be protected when he concludes a contract with a view to purchasing or renting goods or services with a merchant, in the different areas of sale, rental, credit or lending of money and personal purposes. In 1971, the Consumer Protection Office was also created.
See: https://www.opc.gouv.qc.ca/zone-enseignants/liste-activites/activite/droits-responsabilites Accessed 26/8/2024.

Although not binding, it is the first and most important international document including consumer rights on an international scale.

The UNGCP was unanimously approved by the United Nations General Assembly on 9 April 1985. Guidelines differ from treaties, since they are not binding on the parties who have consented to them. While a treaty binds ail parties who have signed, ratified, or approved it, guidelines impose only moral and political obligations. Unanimous approval of the guidelines, however, may contribute to or be evidence of the formation of international customacy law.

The International Organization of Consumer Unions (rocu) initiated activities and extensive lobbying, which led to the adoption of the UNGCP by the United Nations. The rocu encompasses more than 170 leading consumer organizations from more than 60 countries. The activities of rocu to promote the adoption of the guidelines started en 1975 and lasted for 10 years until the resolution was finally adopted by the United Nations.

In 1975, at the rocu World Congress in Australia, a resolution was passed urging 'that the United Nations Secretary-General prepare and issue a report on consumer protection; the United Nations scosoc appointed a group of experts to prepare a Madel Code for Consumer Protection; and the United Nations General Assembly examined and recommended the adoption of that Madel Code by member states of the United Nations. In autumn 1982, after the ECOSOC preparatory work, the first draft of the UNGCP was circulated to various governments for comment. rocu took an active part in the ensuing negotiations and extensive discussions on subsequent drafts of the UNGCP, which led to the consensus resolution and the unanimous adoption of the UNGCP on 9 April 1985 [9].

In 1983, World Consumer Rights Day was celebrated for the first time on March 15, 1983. Each year it provides an opportunity to promote fundamental consumer rights and highlight abuses and social injustices that weaken rights consumers [10].

---

[9] Deutch, Sinai. "Are Consumer Rights Human Rights?" Osgoode Hall Law Journal (1994): 564-565. See: https://digitalcommons.osgoode.yorku.ca/ohlj/vol32/iss3/4
accessed 26/8/2024

[10]See;https://www.opc.gouv.qc.ca/zone-enseignants/listeactivites/activite/droitsresponsabilitesconsommateur/#:~:text=Droit%20%C3%A0%20la%20satisfaction%20des,Droit%20%C3%A0%20un%20environnement%20sain.
Accessed 26/8/2024.

In 1988, the Economic and Social Council of the United Nations adopted a resolution, which encouraged the Member States to implement these guidelines. This not only initiated the discussion on the protection of consumer rights in the area of international law, but above all had an impact on national legislation, often abstracting from this type of regulation[11].

The Charter incorporates the principles of the eight consumer rights and provides a blueprint for strengthening national consumer protection policies. Thanks to the adoption of this Charter, consumer rights were finally elevated to a position of international recognition and legitimacy in both developed and developing countries. However, they may continue to be ignored or denigrated by governments, producers and powerful interests. World Consumer Day draws attention to such violations and promotes a platform for consumer groups to use in countries where they operate [12].

2. Consumer Rights: New Generation of human rights

Despite the international attention that the issue of consumers rights has received at the international level, the problem of considering them a human right remains ambiguous and raises many legal questions?

The biggest problems of consumer protection law, whether consumers are really sufficiently protected by laws based on human rights.

Then a new concept of human rights emerged which included the notion of the right to development or rights to development. The right to or for development includes equality of opportunity for advancement which applies to all nations and includes the rights of everyone who lives as part of the life of that nation. The right to or for this development includes, among others, the right to participate in the development process, and the right to enjoy the results of such development, to enjoy the results of economic, social, and cultural development, education, health, income distribution,

---

[11] Wacinkiewicz, Ewelina Cała "Consumer's Rights as a Special Category of Human Rights," International Journal on Consumer Law and Practice: Vol. 1, Article 2. (2013), p 18. Available at: https://repository.nls.ac.in/ijclp/vol1/iss1/2
accessed 26/8/2024

[12]See:https://www.opc.gouv.qc.ca/zone-enseignants/liste-activites/activite/droits-responsabilites-consommateur/#:~:text=Droit%20%C3%A0%20la%20satisfaction%20des,Droit%20%C3%A0%20un%20environnement%20sain.
Accessed 26/8/2024

employment opportunities, and others, so on. The new conception began to develop en 1986 and is referred to by experts as conceptions of the third generation of human rights[13].

One of the categories of persons whom the international law, including the EU law, as well as particular national laws, granted additional legal protection are consumers and while the very notion of "consumer" has not yet been given a legal definition on the basis of international law[14].

The topic of human rights is not enough to be understood only in the context of vertical power relations, but also includes power relations horizontal, between community groups, between people or groups of people, and even between one community group in a country and another community group. Other countries. Consumer rights in this broad sense can be referred to as a new dimension of human rights that is growing and must be protected from the possibility of abuse or arbitrary action in horizontal power relations between producers and consumers.

Legal protection for consumers is a form of human rights granted by the state. Legal protection for consumers from a human rights perspective is to protect consumer rights. The growing awareness of the state to provide legal protection for consumers from a human rights perspective because they are in a weak bargaining position[15].

As pointed out by J. Sozański "human rights do not exist without economic, social and consumer rights, and without respect for broadly defined human rights one cannot speak of freedom, democracy and the rule of law," which is impossible to disagree with[16].

According to some substantive tests of human rights, consumer rights can be recognized as human rights. These tests, although not conclusive, supply sufficient guidelines in delineating the main features of human rights. The analysis of consumer rights satisfy part of the substantive tests of human rights. Hence, the suggestion to include them as human right base merit.

This suggestion also raises the question of whether new human rights as the third generation of rights should be acknowledged as human rights. The assumption is that

---

[13] Sudanto, Asrizal Saiin, Zaitun, "Legal Protection of Consumer in the Human Rights", Bilancia Vol. 16 No. 1, Januari-Juni (2022), p 5.
[14] Wacinkiewicz, Ewelina Cała, op cit, p17.
[15] Sudanto, Asrizal Saiin, Zaitun, op cit, pp 4-24.
[16] Wacinkiewicz, Ewelina Cała, op cit, p19.

there are three generations of human rights.? Although some writers question the desirability of distinguishing between generations of human rights[17].

Considering how important consumer rights are, thus giving birth to the perception that consumer rights are the Fourth Generation of Human Rights which is the keyword in the conception of human rights in the development of mankind in the future[18].

Characterizing consumer rights - in the light of this assumption - they should be considered as a special category of human rights. They determine the scope of the protection of rights of anyone who in particular relationships will benefit from their consumer status, without limiting at the same time the scope of the exercise of human rights they are entitled to consumers" as the smallest, but also the most numerous economic unit, are important players in the market game in today's economy." This gives sufficient grounds to grant them legal protection in dealing with those who are professionals in the market. Classic human rights are characterized in the object doctrine by a consistent recall of the following characteristics: universality, individual character, inalienability, inviolability and indivisibility[19].

Consumer rights, it seems, have a better chance of being identified as human rights than some of the "new" rights. Rather than being entirely new rights, they are an elaboration and expansion of recognized economic rights. Such recognition, of course, will not be achieved without opposition, and it is possible that it is premature to characterize consumer rights as mandatory human rights. lt is, therefore, advisable to acknowledge them at this stage as "soft" human rights[20]

Assessing consumer rights, or more precisely "the right to protect the interests of consumers," one can assign them a common (universal) character. This means that these rights are universal in nature and are vested in anyone who in defined circumstances acquires consumer status. In addition, the existing laws do not define the delimitation of time allowing the exercise of these rights. And just as we will use the children's rights up to a point, we will, from a certain point (it is easiest to say: with the acquisition of legal capacity) fully benefit from the protection which the law attributes to consumers. Moreover, these rights belong to individual rights. As repeatedly stressed, they are vested in individuals, rather than specific groups, as is the case - for example - of the right of peoples to self-determination. Consumer rights can

[17] Deutch, Sinai. Op cit, p554.

[18] Sudanto, Asrizal Saiin, Zaitun, op cit, pp 5-6.

[19] Wacinkiewicz, Ewelina Cała, op cit, pp 19-20.

[20] Deutch, Sinai. Op cit, p541.

also be attributed the inalienability trait. Interestingly, one may simply not use them, but one cannot renounce them. They are inviolable, which should be interpreted as assigning them legal protection and redress for their violation. They are also indivisible, as being a coherent category they are a whole, enabling comprehensive consumer protection[21].

[21] Wacinkiewicz, Ewelina Cała, op cit, pp 19-20.

Chapter 2.

Development of interest in consumers rights in European laws and some countries in the world

The topic of interest in consumer rights has witnessed a great development in modern legislation, and this was especially evident in European legislation that was influenced by American legislation regarding the establishment and protection of consumer rights. Which made the issue of consumer rights occupy a large position in Europe, especially in the United Kingdom, France, Italy and Spain, which knew great interest in consumers rights, as was evident in its legislation (**I**).

Most countries of the world have also kept pace with the movement of interest in consumers rights. In Asia, for example, interest in consumer rights emerged in China at the beginning of the nineties, where China experienced an economic renaissance accompanied by the development of interest in consumer rights, especially in light of the digital transformation that China has experienced. This is also the example in the Arab countries that It witnessed radical changes in its economies and adopted policies of A market economy based on economic freedoms, which made it give a status to consumers in order to preserve their rights (**II**).

I. The development of interest in consumers rights in European laws

Thanks to the efforts of jurisprudence and the judiciary, which have contributed greatly to the development of interest in consumer rights and their judicial and legislative applications, the topic of consumer rights in Europe has received great attention thanks to the efforts of jurisprudence and the judiciary, which have contributed a major role, and this has been demonstrated in the legislative system that the European Union has established since 1985. Despite the UK withdrawal from the European Union (**1**).

In addition to the French legislator, which is considered a model for national European legislation in the field of protecting consumer rights as a result of the great development witnessed by the legislative system in France. The same applies to Italy and Spain (**2**).

1. The development of interest in consumers rights in European and UK law

The issue of interest in consumer rights has received great attention since the eighties of the last century, and this was evident in the legislative texts issued by the European Union in this regard, which constituted a reference for the legislation of European countries(**A**), with the exception of the United Kingdom, which withdrew from the European Union(**B**).

A. The development of interest in consumers rights in European law

European countries' interest in the topic of consumer rights began in the early 1980s as part of their adoption of the European Common Market. The European Parliament has enacted several directives with the aim of achieving legislative harmony between various European countries on the issue of consumer rights.

The first directive was promulgated by the European Union en 1985 under No: 85-577 promulgated on December 20, 1985, relating to consumer protection in contracts outside commercial centres, then Directive No.: 97-07 issued on May 20, 1997 relating to consumer protection in distance contracting, which was repealed en 2011, pursuant to Directive No: 2011-83 of October 25, 2011 relating to consumer rights, which amended Directive No: 93-13 as well as Directive No.: 1999-44. These efforts came in order to ensure that the European Union contributes to establishing a high level of protection for consumers in the application of articles 114 and 169 of the European Union Agreement, and this is in light of respect for fundamental rights, especially the principles stipulated in the Charter of Fundamental Rights of the European Union, as indicated in Paragraph 66 of the European Directive for 2011[22].

Some writers have addressed the question of how the provisions of this directive are implemented by national legislation in light of the specificity of the consumer environment in the European Union, especially UK, which has exited from this space?

---

[22] Directive 2011/83/EU of the European Parliament and of the Council of 25 October 2011 on consumer rights, amending Council Directive 93/13/EEC and Directive 1999/44/EC of the European Parliament and of the Council and repealing Council Directive 85/577/EEC and Directive 97/7/EC of the European Parliament and of the Council Text with EEA relevance
See: https://eur-lex.europa.eu/legal-content/EN/TXT/?uri=celex%3A32011L0083
Accessed 26/8/2024.

EU law has brought some changes to consumer rights, notably in the context of remedies; the introduction of the Consumer Sales Directive has not marked, as Dirk Staudenmayer had hoped, 'an important step towards a future private European law[23].

Others have also discussed the concept of the average consumer, on the basis of which consumer rights are determined to be protected in the EU.

Where the standard for the average consumer adopted in Directives aiming to approximate the private laws of the Member States is markedly different from the EU law 'average consumer'. Rather than tailoring rules to the well-informed, circumspect consumer, these Directives introduce rights and remedies that go well beyond what is necessary for the protection of this group (however diverse it may be). Instead, information requirements, rights of withdrawal and ex officio protection of consumers ensure that even the most nonchalant consumer can claim protection if he wants it[24].

The European judiciary also contributed to strengthening the protection of consumer rights and establishing effective protection for them, especially against unfair clauses, by seeking to achieve harmony with the legal systems in the European Union. The contributions of European jurisprudence were evident in recognizing the existence of a common European law of contracts, as well as highlighting the concept of positive obligation, as well as recognizing the responsibility In the event that the state breaches this obligation based on the idea of contractual solidarity.

In light of the vitality of European human rights law and its connection to the contractual field, despite the failure of the European judiciary to recognize the European Union Charter on fundamental rights, which has raised a lot of controversy and ambiguity about clarifying the nature of the relationship that exists between fundamental rights. Market law, as well as the position of the European judiciary [25].

---

[23] Giliker, P." The Consumer Rights Act 2015 - a bastion of European consumer rights? Legal Studies", publisher policies. (2017). pp 13-29.
http://www.bristol.ac.uk/red/research-policy/pure/user-guides/ebr-terms/

[24] Vanessa Mak, Standards of Protection," In Search of the 'Average Consumer' of EU Law in the Proposal for a Consumer Rights Directive", TISCO, European Review of Private Law, No 04, juin(2010), p 6.
https://www.researchgate.net/publication/228223696

[25] Mathieu Combe, "On the use of the Charters of Fundamental Rights in the Fight against unfair clauses in contracts", Lamy Business Law Review, n° 100 (2006): 48-52.

This was clearly demonstrated in his latest jurisprudence issued on September 10, 2014 in the case of C – 34/13 Kusionova[26].

Nowadays, the EU's consumer protection policy ensures the preservation of their interests in many areas, ranging from the fight against unfair commercial practices to false advertising, including the regulation of product labeling and protection of travelers' rights.

In November 2020, the European Commission adopted its new consumer agenda, its overall vision of EU consumer protection for the period 2020-2025. This document thus sets out the priority areas in this area: the ecological transition, digital transformation, the effective application of consumer rights, the specific needs of certain consumer groups and international cooperation. This European approach focused on consumers, and not only on producers, has resulted in concrete progress in many areas.

In recent years, the European Union has strengthened consumer rights in terms of purchases. Europeans now benefit from a minimum two-year warranty on all products, requiring merchants to repair, replace or refund them. As well as a period of 14 days during which buyers can cancel their order or return it without any justification. Since 2003, a European rapid alert system has allowed Member States to exchange

---

[26] The facts of this case are that Ms Kušionová from Slovenia entered into a consumer loan contract on 26 February 2009 with the German SMART Capital in the amount of €10,000, arranging a mortgage on her family home as security for the loan. Ms. Kušionová filed a lawsuit against SMART Capital with the Okresný súd Humenné District Court to cancel the consumer loan contract as well as the mortgage contract, citing the unfair clauses binding her.
This court of first instance partially annulled the loan contract due to some unfair clauses, but the parties appealed this ruling to Krajský súd v Prešove (Prešove Regional Court), which noted that the unfair clause was derived from a legal text, namely Article 151 of the Civil Code.
Following the referral, European jurisprudence held that the provisions of European Directive: 93/13/EEC of 5 April 1993 on arbitrary terms in contracts concluded with consumers must be interpreted in a way that does not conflict with national legislation relating to the recovery of debts based on unfair clause, and therefore must be interpreted Article 1 (2) of Directive 93/13 provides that a contractual term appearing in a contract concluded by a professional with a consumer falls outside the scope of application of this Directive if this unfair clause is derived from a mandatory legislative or regulatory provision. See:
https://curia.europa.eu/juris/document/document.jsf;jsessionid=2AA41CA8AAB4C25673D7A2F479490725?text=&docid=157486&pageIndex=0&doclang=FR&mode=lst&dir=&occ=first&part=1&cid=837733
Accessed 7/7/2024.

information on products presenting a risk to the health and safety of consumers and to take coordinated measures[27].

New dispositions are also expected to come, like a right to repair on which Parliament voted on April 23, 2024 in plenary session. After its formal adoption by the Council of the EU and transposition by member states, it will require manufacturers to repair household products such as washing machines or vacuum cleaners. Another directive should also make it possible to prohibit misleading ecological claims on packaging (or "greenwashing") and guarantee information on the repairability of objects. When they travel within the European Union. Since 2017, roaming charges have been abolished, allowing Europeans to make calls, send SMS and go online anywhere in the EU. Similar rules allow access to paid content online (online television, e-books, games, music) in another Member State. To travel more easily, the rights of air transport passengers, but also those of rail transport, have been gradually extended [28].

B. The development of interest in consumers rights in UK law

The Consumer Rights Act 2015 is a landmark legislation in the area of consumer protection in the UK. This particular legislation strives to streamline, strengthen and modernize the overall consumer protection regime in the UK. This legislation would play a vital role in harmonization and consolidation of consumer laws in the UK and would result in effective protection of consumer rights[29].

It has been described by consumer organisation Which? as 'the biggest shake up in consumer rights law in a generation'. Its aims are ambitious: to simplify, strengthen and modernise UK consumer law, consolidating in one place fundamental consumer rights covering contracts for goods, services, digital content and the law relating to unfair terms in consumer contracts. These goals are impressive and respond to genuine consumer needs UK consumer law, prior to the Act, was unnecessarily complex

---

[27]Article Published by Valentin Ledroit, See: outeleurope.eu/l-europe-et-moi/comment-l-union-europeenne-assure-t-elle-la-protection-des-consommateurs/#:~:text=Ces%20dernières%20années%2C%20l'Union,les%20remplacer%20ou%20les%20rembourser. accessed 25/08/2024.

[28] Ibid

[29] Muhammad Akbar Khan," The Origin and Development of Consumer Protection Laws", Journal of Asian and African Social Scienceand Humanities, Vol. 3, No. 3, (2017), p 44. https://www.aarcentre.com/ojs3/index.php/jaash/article/view/127/342 Accessed 28/09/2024.

fragmented and, in places, unclear, for example where the law had not kept up with technological change, lacked precision or was couched in legalistic language.

A key reason for this complexity has been the introduction into UK law over the past 30 years of new consumer rights deriving from European directives. Such measures have, in the main, been transposed into UK law using the 'copy out' approach, by which the draftsman, whenever possible, reproduces the wording of the directive usually [30].

Looking at Part 1 of the Act, while EU law has brought some changes to consumer rights, notably in the context of remedies, the introduction of the Consumer Sales Directive has not marked, as Dirk Staudenmayer had hoped, 'an important step towards a future private European law'. Rather the UK government has concentrated on ensuring that the minimum necessary adjustment to national law is achieved. The measures contained in the Consumer Rights Directive are relegated to low profile secondary legislation and we might further reflect on the wisdom of not including all the provisions of a maximum harmonisation directive focused on consumer rights in a major UK statute dealing with consumer rights. We might question also to what extent the EU measures, despite the restructuring process, continue to act as what Teubner would term 'legal irritants', fitting uncomfortably with existing measures. Signposting does not signify that the different directions make sense collectively.

The fact that the insertion of the CSD into the CRA is described by the Government itself as 'adequate' suggests that this is not an overwhelming endorsement of EU consumer policy. What we see is a consolidation of (some) UK consumer law, taking into account EU directives, in a manner that does little to advance the cause for harmonising consumer rights and remedies across the EU. On this basis, it is unlikely that post-Brexit the UK government will engage in the time and effort to excise the provisions of the CSD from UK law, denying consumers rights and remedies with which they are now familiar. This suggests that Part 1 of the Act is likely to continue in its current form. The real focus of Part1 is the creation of a domestically coherent framework for UK consumer rights[31].

UK seeks to simplify, strengthen and modernise consumer law and to resolve inconsistencies and overlaps caused by the implementation of EU legislation in domestic law. The decision to absorb and consolidate a number of EU directives must,

---

[30] Giliker, P. op cit, pp1-2.

[31] Ibid, p28.

however, now be considered in the light of the decision in the June 2016 referendum that the UK should withdraw from the EU [32].

Although, most EU law applicable in the UK as at 31 December 2020 remains in effect within the UK indefinitely as "retained EU law" (unless or until the Government decides to repeal or amend it). This new body of retained EU law includes a raft of consumer protection measures.

The primary focus of both SIs is on the enforcement of consumer rights both in the UK and in the EU post-Brexit. Both SIs have applied since 1 January 2021. Specifically, the purpose of the "Protection Regulations" is to:

- remove or amend references to EU law from consumer legislation, to ensure that it continues to operate effectively now the UK has left the EU.
- make further amendments to clarify that, from the end of the transition period, consumer contracts concerned with imports from EEA countries will be treated in the same way as contracts dealing with imports from non-EEA countries.

Affected consumer legislation includes:

- Consumer Rights Act 2015
- Consumer Protection from Unfair Trading Regulations 2008 (SI 2008/1277)
- Consumer Rights (Payment Surcharges) Regulations 2012 (SI 2012/3110)
- Consumer Contracts (Information, Cancellation and Additional Charges) Regulations 2013 (SI 2013/3134)
- Alternative Dispute Resolution for Consumer Disputes (Competent Authorities and Information) Regulations 2015 (SI 2015/542). The purpose of the "Enforcement Regulations" is to either remove or amend references to EU legislation in relation to the enforcement of various consumer protection laws [33].

[32] Giliker, P. op cit p30.

[33] Lorraine Conway, "Brexit: UK consumer protection law", Commons Library Briefing, 21 May (2021), pp4-6.

2. The development of interest in consumer rights in French, Italian and Spanish law.

The countries of the European Union have followed the movement of interest in consumer rights, following the example of European legislation and European policy in the field of interest in consumer rights. This is what appeared, for example, in France(**A**), Italy(**B**), and Spain(**C**).

A. The development of interest in consumers rights in French law

Most European countries have sought to pay attention to consumer rights and enhance their protection and enshrine them within their internal legislative system, the most prominent of which is France, under which the French consumer law underwent several amendments, the most important of which is the 2014 amendment, which reflected the government's goals in establishing a new mechanism for economic regulation. In order to restore the Balancing contractual positions between Consumers and professionals, achieving a kind of justice between economic actors and restoring confidence and credit to consumers as an effective element in economic recovery, Law: 2014-344 promulgated on March 17, 2014 (Hamon law) came to enhance consumer protection for professionals through all stages of contracting (before, during, and upon contract implementation), support oversight mechanisms, review the deterrent aspect, and tighten penalties[34] .

The French legislator also included another amendment to the consumer law in 2015 under Law: 2015-990 promulgated on August 6, 2015 relating to growth, activity and equal economic opportunities (Macron Law), through which the French legislator included several fundamental corrections regarding the basic techniques for consumer protection , which are the obligation to inform before contracting, the consumer's right to withdraw, and the exclusion of unfair clauses, and this is in order to in order to harmonize them with European Directive No. 2011-53 promulgated on October 25, 2011[35].

In parallel, the French consumer law has witnessed several attempts at codification since the 1993, despite the amendments it introduced, until the 2016. The

---

[34] Chloé Minet, "Hamon Law; Is Better the Enemy of Good?" Lamy Business Law Review, n° 93 (May 2014): 44.

[35] Natacha Sauphanor - Brouilland, "The impact of the Macron Law on Contractual Consumer Law", Contract Review, (March 2016): 97.

date of promulgate of law: 2016-301 on March 14, 2016, which restructured the aspects of the consumer law, whether related to the conclusion of the contract or its execution to implement. In addition to the private disposition for some contracts as well as distance contracts, this order introduced fundamental amendments to the legislative aspect of consumer law with the aim of protecting the consumer and in order to harmonize with European legislation. This issue is considered inevitable and unavoidable in order to reach a fixed, permanent, and codified law[36].

After 2016, the French Consumer Law underwent several successive amendments, the most recent of which was pursuant to law No. 2021-1247 promulgated on September 29, 2021, in addition to other amendments made to its provisions in 2024 under special texts, all of which aim to protect and enhance the rights of consumers in France, in particular. Within the framework of digital transactions[37].

B. The development of interest in consumers rights in Italian law.

Italy has a robust framework of consumer protection laws and regulations aimed at safeguarding the rights and interests of consumers. These regulations are designed to ensure transparency, fairness, and safety in consumer transactions.

Consumer Code (Codice del Consumo): The Consumer Code is the cornerstone of consumer protection in Italy. It comprehensively covers various aspects of consumers rights and obligations. It regulates issues such as product safety, warranties, distance selling, and unfair commercial practices[38].

---

[36] Sabine Bernheim-Desvaux and Guy Raymond, "Crossed Perspectives on the Reform of the legislative part of the Consumer Code", Consumer Competition Contracts Review (August-September 2016):7.

[37] See the most important amendments to the French consumer law:

- Decree No. 2024-753 of July 7, 2024 amending the Consumer Code with regard to the information obligations of providers of online comparators, online marketplaces and online news content aggregators
- Law No. 2024-449 of May 21, 2024 aimed at securing and regulating the digital space.
- Law No. 2004-575 of June 21, 2004 for confidence in the digital economy.

See: https://www.legifrance.gouv.fr/codes/texte_lc/LEGITEXT000006069565/
(accessed 26/08/2024).

[38]See:https://globalregulatoryinsights.com/insight/comprehensive-analysis-consumer-protection-laws-in-italy-2023/
Accessed 26/08/2024.

Consumers' rights are safeguarded in Italy by provisions in the Civil Code and in Legislative Decree No. 206 of 6 September 2005, implementing EC Directive No: 29/2005. As a result of Legislative Decree No: 146 of 2 August 2007, implementing Directive No: 2005/29/EC concerning unfair business-to-consumer commercial practices in the internal market and amending Directive No: 84/450/EEC, 97/7/EC, 98/27/EC, 2002/65/EC and Regulation (EC) No: 2006/2004. The ICA is responsible for the enforcement of the Code in relation to unfair business-to-consumer practices carried out before, during and after a commercial transaction.

This chapter concerns the enforcement of the Code rules by the ICA in relation to business-to-consumer commercial practices; it does not consider the rules on contracts entered into by consumers, which, pursuant to Section 1469-bis of the Civil Code, are governed by the general provisions of the Civil Code (Title II), unless amended by the specific consumer protection rules introduced in Italy by the Code, or by other rules that are more favourable to the consumer[39].

The principal consumer protection laws and regulations in Italy include:

Product Safety Regulations: Italy, like the European Union, adheres to strict product safety standards. Products sold in Italy must meet safety requirements, and manufacturers and distributors are obliged to report any unsafe products. The Italian Ministry of Economic Development is responsible for overseeing product safety.

Distance Selling Regulations: These regulations govern e-commerce transactions, ensuring that consumers receive clear information about products and their rights when making online purchases. Consumers have a right to cancel orders within a specified period and receive a refund.

Unfair Commercial Practices: Italy prohibits unfair commercial practices, including misleading advertising and aggressive sales tactics. The Consumer Code sets out rules for transparent advertising and marketing practices.

Consumer Guarantees: Consumers in Italy are entitled to statutory guarantees on the products they purchase. These guarantees cover defects, conformity with the

[39] Written by a member of ICLG's international panel of experts, Consumer Protection Laws and Regulations Italy 2024,
See: https://iclg.com/practice-areas/consumer-protection-laws-and-regulations/italy
Accessed 26/08/2024.

contract, and the duration of warranties. The law mandates that sellers provide clear information on warranties and how to make warranty claims.

Consumer Rights in contracts: The Consumer Code regulates the content and format of consumer contracts, ensuring that they are clear and easily understandable. Consumers must be informed about the terms and conditions, including cancellation and return policies.

Alternative Dispute Resolution (ADR) and Online Dispute Resolution (ODR): Italy promotes ADR mechanisms to resolve disputes between consumers and businesses without going to court. The ODR platform provided by the European Commission allows consumers and traders to resolve disputes related to online purchases through an online platform.

Consumer Associations: Consumer associations play a vital role in representing consumers' interests and can take legal action on behalf of consumers. They are empowered to challenge unfair practices and seek remedies for affected consumers.

Data Protection: While not specific to consumer protection, data protection regulations, such as the General Data Protection Regulation (GDPR), also benefit consumers by safeguarding their personal data and privacy.

Tourism Regulations: Italy, being a popular tourist destination, has regulations governing the tourism industry. These regulations ensure that tourists are provided with accurate information about services, prices, and cancellation policies.

It is important to note that Italy, as a member of the European Union, also adheres to EU directives and regulations related to consumer protection, which complement and enhance the national consumer protection framework.

In conclusion, Italy has a comprehensive set of consumer protection laws and regulations that cover various aspects of consumer transactions. These laws aim to protect consumers from unfair practices, ensure product safety, and promote transparency and fairness in the marketplace. Consumers in Italy can rely on these regulations to assert their rights and seek remedies in case of disputes or issues with products and services [40].

---

[40] See: https://globalregulatoryinsights.com/insight/comprehensive-analysis-consumer-protection-laws-in-italy-2023/
Accessed 26/08/2024.

C. The development of interest in consumers rights in Spanish law.

The protection of consumers in Spain and users is a basic principle under which the State is required to guarantee citizens their rights and freedoms in this area.

Article 51 of the Spanish Constitution (Abre en nueva ventana) requires public authorities to ensure the protection of consumers and users, to protect their safety, health and economic interests, to promote information and education for consumers and users and to support consumer and user organisations[41].

The recast General Law for the Defence of Consumers (Royal-Legislative Decree 1/2007, of 16 November, or "GLDC") contains the essential rules and regulations regarding consumer rights in Spain. Other relevant pieces of legislation that co-exist with the GLDC include:

Royal Decree on General Product Safety (Royal Decree 1801/2003, of 26 December), or (LGPS):

- Law on Unfair Competition (Law 3/1991, of 10 January), or (LUC).
- Law on General Conditions in Contracts (Law 7/1998, of 13 April).
- Regulation on Transparency and the Protection of Banking Services Customers (Order EHA/2899/2011, of 28 October).
- Law on Real Estate Loans (Law 5/2019, of 9 March).

Consumers have a basic general right to be protected against risks to their health and safety, as well as risks against their legitimate social and economic interest. There are substantive tests related to the conformity with consumer legislation of goods and digital content and services[42].

Following the recent implementation into the Spanish laws of Directives 2019/770 and 2019/771, the Government is making new legislative efforts driven by European initiatives to update the consumer protection laws. Specifically, the Government published on 2 July 2021 a draft bill (the "Draft Bill") to implement Directive 2019/2161 (also known as the "Omnibus Directive") into the Spanish laws, which represents the main body of the New Deal for Consumers. According to the timeline set by the Omnibus Directive. The Draft Bill incorporates the provisions of

[41] See:https://administracion.gob.es/pag_Home/en/Tu-espacio-europeo/derechos-obligaciones/empresas/inicio-gestion-cierre/practicas-comerciales/derechos-consumidores.html (accessed 27/08/2024).

[42] See: https://iclg.com/practice-areas/consumer-protection-laws-and-regulations/spain Accessed 27/08/2024.

the Omnibus Directive with a few particularities, thereby updating the amendments made by the latter (among others) to the Directives on unfair commercial practices, on consumer rights, and on the indication of prices of products offered to the consumers[43].

Royal Decree-Law 7/2021, 27 April, transposed Directive (EU) 2019/770 and Directive (EU) 2019/771 into the Consolidated Text of the General Law for the Defence of Consumers and Users. This new regulation entered into force 1 January 2022. The new features introduced are related to the guarantee regime and, specifically, to the conformity of goods, remedies for lack of conformity and deadlines. So, the RDL 7/2021, is characterised by providing reinforced consumer protection in terms of guarantees and after-sales services in comparison with the current legislation in force[44].

In addition, Protection against risks to their health or safety is one of the basic rights of consumers, goods and services placed on the market must therefore be safe, they must not, under normal or reasonably foreseeable conditions, pose any health or safety risk to persons. Also according to Royal Decree 1801/2003(Abre en nueva ventana) , both producers and distributors have a duty to ensure that only safe products are placed on the market and sold. Producer means a manufacturer if it is established in the European Union, or a manufacturer that affixes its name, trade mark or other distinguishing feature, the manufacturer's representative or the other professionals in the marketing chain in so far as its activities may affect the safety characteristics of the product[45].

I. The emergence of interest in consumers rights in some countries of the world

Interest in consumer rights has begun to appear in most countries of the world. In Asia, the Chinese legislator promulgated legislation on consumer rights in 1994 because of growing awareness of the need to pay attention to consumer rights. In the

---

[43]See:https://www.osborneclarke.com/insights/updating-consumer-protection-laws-spain-implementation-omnibus-directive
Accessed 27/08/2024.

[44]See: https://e-justice.europa.eu/37165/EN/enforcement?SPAIN&member=1
(accessed 27/08/2024).

[45]See :https://administracion.gob.es/pag_Home/en/Tu-espacio-europeo/derechos-obligaciones/empresas/inicio-gestion-cierre/practicas-comerciales/derechos-consumidores.html
Accessed 27/08/2024.

same effort, Indonesia in 1999 promulgated legislation to protect consumer rights, which indicates growing awareness of consumer rights. In Asia (**1**).

Consumer protection legislation has also witnessed major developments in the Arab countries especially in Algeria in light of the latter's efforts to establish effective protection for consumer rights as rights resulting from developments in modern economic life in light of the market economy (**2**).

3. The emergence of interest in consumers rights in china and Indonesia

China and Indonesia represent the largest category of consumers in Asia, and their legislative system has witnessed development in the field of concern for consumer rights.

A- The emergence of interest in consumers rights in china

Chinese consumer law resides mainly in the "Consumer Protection Law" which came into application in 1994[46]. Consumer rights protection has also been strengthened in the new law of October 25, 2012 which came into application on March 15, 2014[47].

The new Law has integrated into its system rules ,which aim to protect the rights and legitimate interests of consumers, in particular the rights concerning consumers' personal data, and the right to return products, which do not meet quality requirements. As well as the right to reliable information on the price and place of production, manufacturer, use, performance, specifications, quality, main ingredients, date of

[46] Consumer Rights Protection Law of the People's Republic of China, see articles 7 to 15 of the Consumer Protection Act, See:
https://www.wipo.int/wipolex/fr/legislation/details/8745
accessed 24/8/2024

[47] Alina Quach, Report of the November 19, 2014 meeting of the Paris-Beijing/China International Commission of the Paris Bar, See:
https://www.lagbd.org/Produire_et_distribuer_en_Chine_:_le_renforcement_de_la_protection_des_consommateurs_(cn)#II._La_nouvelle_loi_de_protection_des_droit_des_consommateurs_du_25_octobre_2012_.28en_vigueur_le_15_mars_2014.29
Accessed 24/8/2024.

production, validity period, certificate of inspection, user guide, after-sales services, specifications and service charges[48].

The operator must provide the consumer with accurate and complete information on the quality, performance, purpose and validity period of its products or services, and may not make any false or misleading advertising. It must clearly indicate the real name and brand [49].

B- The emergence of interest in consumers rights in Indonesia

The protection and enforcement of human rights in Indonesia is still half-hearted. One aspect of human rights that has not been touched properly in the protection and enforcement of human rights is consumer protection. Whatever it is, the significance of regulating consumers rights in Indonesia is through Law Number 8 of 1999 concerning Consumer Protection (UUPK). This law is part of its implementation as a welfare state because the 1945 Constitution in addition to being a political constitution can also be called an economic constitution, namely a constitution that contains the idea of a welfare state that has grown and developed due to the influence of socialism since the nineteenth century.

In addition, the existence of UUPK is a milestone in the development of consumer protection law in Indonesia.

Law No. 8 of 1999 regulates consumer protection policies, whether with regard to the material law or the formal law regarding consumer dispute resolution.

The importance of legal protection for consumers is due to the weak bargaining position of consumers. Legal protection for consumers requires siding with a weak bargaining position (consumers).

In the end, as a system, the implementation of legal protection for consumers cannot be separated from the context of national development. It can be said that there

---

[48] Alina Quach, op cit, See:
https://www.lagbd.org/Produire_et_distribuer_en_Chine_:_le_renforcement_de_la_protection_des_consommateurs_(cn)#II._La_nouvelle_loi_de_protection_des_droit_des_consommateurs_du_25_octobre_2012_.28en_vigueur_le_15_mars_2014.29
Accessed 24/8/2024

[49] Ibid

is an integrated concept in the Consumer Protection Act (UUPK), in the implementation of legal protection for consumers [50].

4. The emergence of interest in consumers rights in the Arab countries and Algeria

Interest in the topic of consumer rights has begun to emerge in some Arab countries, especially Algeria, and this is a result of its modern economic trends and the manifestations of economic globalization that economic life has witnessed in Arab countries. Most Arab countries sought to adopt protective legislation for consumer rights, in keeping with the movement of international interest in consumer rights (**A**).

Algeria also paid special attention to the rights of consumers, and this was embodied in its constitution, as Algeria was considered one of the Arab countries that worked to stipulate the rights of consumers within its constitution(**B**).

A. The emergence of interest in consumers rights in the some of Arab countries

Despite the international interest in consumer rights at the beginning of the eighties of the last century, most Arab countries did not embody this interest within their legislative systems, especially within their constitutions, as consumer protection remained derived from the rules of civil law, even though the constitutions of the Arab countries paid attention to basic rights and codified them within their constitutions.

For example, the Tunisian constitutional establishment did not stipulate economic rights, nor even consumer rights, despite the policy of economic openness adopted within the Tunisian Constitution promulgated on January 26, 2014[51] .

This is also the same situation with the Moroccan Constitution, despite the series of amendments that it underwent over the: 1962 - 1972 - 1992 - 1996[52]. with the exception of what the Moroccan Constitution of 2011 referred to in Chapter 36 of it to

---

[50] Sudanto, Asrizal Saiin, Zaitun, op cit, pp 2-12.

[51] See the Tunisian Constitution issued on January 26, 2014.

[52] See the Moroccan Constitution of 2011.

practices that violate the principles of free and legitimate competition in economic relations without explicitly stipulating Protecting consumers' rights.

The same situation applies to the Mauritanian Constitution issued in 1991 under Legal Order: 028-91[53], which referred in its preamble to economic and social rights, as the Mauritanian founder contented himself with stipulating freedom of trade and industry and considered them among the basic rights within Article 10.

Otherwise, in Kuwait, the Kuwaiti Constitution referred in Article 20 to Kuwait's endeavour to raise the level of welfare and achieve prosperity for citizens[54] .

The amended Egyptian Constitution on April 23, 2019 touched upon Article 27 of the Egyptian Constitution stipulating consumer protection[55]. which indicates the interest of the Egyptian constitutional founder in the topic of protecting consumer rights, and this is what the Egyptian legislator enshrined within the Consumer Protection Law No. 181 of 2018.

Although the Syrian Constitution did not address consumer rights within the Syrian Constitution. But the Syrian legislator stipulated consumer rights within the text of Article 2 of Law No. 14 of 2015 AD on Internal Trade and Consumer Protection promulgated on July 26, 2015, where Article 2 stipulates: "This law aims to ensure the practice of economic activity for all, prevent monopoly, and protect consumer rights....".[56]

The State of Qatar has also made great efforts to concretize and protect the rights of the consumers in the Law No: (8) of 2008 regarding consumer protection, amended and supplemented in 2018, in this context, the Qatari Consumer Protection Law is considered one of the modern legislations that explicitly stipulates consumer rights, as indicated in Article (2) of Law No. (8) of 2008 regarding consumer protection[57].

---

[53] The Mauritanian Constitution issued in 1991 pursuant to Legal order: 028-91.

[54] However, the Kuwaiti legislator addressed the issue of protecting consumers rights within Article 9 of Law No. 39 of 2014 related to consumer protection, See http://www.law.gov.kw/KWT_LC- accessed 03/05/2024.

[55] The Egyptian Constitution amended on April 23, 2019, https://manshurat.org/node/14675 accessed 03/05/2024.

[56] The Syrian Constitution. See: http://pministry.gov.sy/contents/12332/ accessed 03/05/2024.

[57] Law on Consumer Protection, Qatar, No. (8) of 2008 amended by Decree Law No. (14) of 2011, and Law No. (7) of 2018, See: https://almeezan.qa/LawView.aspx?opt&LawID=2528&language=ar. Accessed 03/05/2024.

Thus, the Qatari legislator has explicitly stipulated the rights of consumers guaranteed by law, which constitute guarantees for the consumer in his contractual relationships that he concludes with suppliers and various providers of products and services in view of the economic superiority and know-how that he and the providers possess in contrast to consumers[58].

As for the UAE legislator promulgated Federal Law No. 15 of 2020 regarding consumer protection, which considered one of the modern Arab legislations that explicitly stipulates consumer rights, as stated in Article 4 of Federal Law No. 15 of 2020[59].

Accordingly, most Arab legislation is among the modern legislation that has kept pace with the legislative interest in consumer rights, and they are also required to embody this interest within their constitutions in order to enhance the legal protection of consumer rights.

B- The emergence of interest in consumers rights in Algeria

Algeria began to pay attention to consumer rights in 1989 in the context of adopting a market economy enshrined in the 1989 Constitution, where the first legislation containing general rules for consumer protection was enacted under Law

---

[58] Sami Benhamla, "Legislative Attention in Consumers' Rights, a New Approach within Modern Legislations: Qatari and Algerian Legislations as Models", p 53.

[59] Article 4 of Federal Law No. 15 of 2020 stipulates the following:
All obligations stipulated under this law are considered rights of consumers, including:
1. Providing an appropriate and safe environment when purchasing a product or receiving a service.
2. Obtaining the correct information about the goods he buys, uses or consumes or the service he receives.
3. Educating and making him aware of his rights and obligations.
4. Exercising his rights to choose the most appropriate product and service available in the market according to his desire.
5. Protecting the privacy and security of its data when using it for promotional and marketing purposes.
6. Respect his religious values, customs and traditions when providing him with any good or receiving any service.
7. Fair and prompt settlement of his disputes.
8. Obtaining fair compensation for the damage caused to him or his money as a result of purchasing the product, using it, or receiving the service.
9. All other rights stipulated by the legislation in force in the country.
Any other rights may be added by a decision of the Council of Ministers."

No. 89-02 promulgated on February 7, 1989[60]. Then, in 2004, the Algerian legislator issued Law: 04-02 on June 23, 2004, which specifies the rules applied to commercial practices, as amended in 2010, which included rules to protect the consumer from unfair and arbitrary commercial practices[61].

In 2009, the Algerian legislator promulgated new law related to consumer protection and the suppression of fraud N: 09-03 issued on February 25, 2009, amended in 2015 and 2018[62], through which the Algerian legislator clarified a set of obligations that fall on the intervener and which are matched by consumer rights. The most important of which is the obligation to inform and ensure the security and safety of products. Monitoring, ensuring defects, and ensuring the material and moral interests of the consumer, in addition to highlighting the role of consumer protection associations and advisory bodies that he established.

The Algerian legislator was not satisfied with this legislative and regulatory arsenal, but rather worked to constitutionalize consumer rights in 2016 within the constitutional amendment issued under Law 16-01 issued on March 6, 2016, within Article 43 of it, which considered consumer rights as part of the economic rights that fall within basic rights. It stipulates the following: "... **The State guarantees the regulation of market and the law protects the rights of consumers**".

However, within the framework of the new constitutional amendment of 2020, the content of the Article 43 was changed to be replaced by Article 62, which stipulates: "**Public authorities shall work to protect the consumer, in a way that guarantees them security, safety, health, and their economic rights**".[63]

Although the Algerian legislator and the Algerian Constitution did not specify the content of these rights, the Algerian Constitution is considered one of the Arab constitutions that was quick to constitutionalize consumer rights in a way that enhances

---

[60] Law relating to general rules for consumer protection, Algeria, No.: 89-02 dated the first of Rajab in the year 1409 corresponding to February 7, 1989.

[61] Law defining the rules applicable to commercial practices Commercial Practices, Algeria, No. 04-02 of 5 Jumada al-Awwal 1425 corresponding to June 23, 2004, amended and supplemented by Law 10-06 issued on August 15, 2010.

[62] Law relating to consumer protection and suppression of fraud, Algeria, No.: 09-03 issued on Safar 29, 1430 AH, corresponding to February 25, 2009, amended by the Supplementary Finance Law 2015. And the law of 2018.

[63] Law Containing the Constitutional Amendment of 2020, Algeria, No. 82 issued on December 30, 2020.

the legal protection of consumers' interests through its approval of constitutional protection[64].

In the end, the interest of Arab legislators in consumer rights is evident as long as the consumer has become a primary actor in the modern economic approach, and this is what achieves and enhances security and confidence for the consumer group by ensuring an appropriate economic environment that achieves effective protection of consumer rights and works to improve their livelihood.

[64] Sami Benhamla, "Legislative Attention in Consumers' Rights, a New Approach within Modern Legislations: Qatari and Algerian Legislations as Models", pp 55-56.

Section 2.

The content of consumers rights and the role of competition law in promoting them

Consumer rights, in terms of content and the nature of the rights associated with the consumer category, have developed thanks to the efforts of jurisprudence, politicians, economists, and jurists. Consumer rights include the right to the right to safety, the right to be informed, the right to choose, the right to be heard the right to redress, the right to consumer education, the right to a healthy environment.

The promotion of these rights is also linked to the extent of the effectiveness of competition legislation in maintaining competition in the market, so that improving the lives of consumers is considered one of the most important goals of competition legislation that the latter seeks to achieve.

Chapter 1.

Consumer rights content

The content of consumers' rights witnessed a development that coincided with the development of the interest that this new category of rights received, as jurisprudence, politicians, and jurisprudence played a major role in highlighting these rights **(I)** and clarifying their content **(II).**

I. Evolution of the content of consumers rights

The catalogue of consumers rights has not yet been drawn up. The reasons for this state of affairs must be considered mainly in the dissimilarities of national legal systems, which result in a lack of consensus on the international scene, concerning, among other things, the list of rights, which set a minimum standard of protection deserving of, be carried out legally[65].

Nevertheless, during a speech of John F. Kennedy before the American Congress in 1962: the originally formulated consumer rights directory contained four basic rights:

B. the right to safety,
C. the right to information,
D. the right to choose products and services at competitive prices and
E. the right of expression of opinions influencing the development of consumer policy.

The global consumer federation Consumers International subsequently improved this list by adding four other rights:

F. Right to satisfaction of basic needs.
G. Right to repair.
H. Consumer right to education.
I. Right to a healthy environment[66].

---

[65] Wacinkiewicz, Ewelina Cała, op cit, p20.

[66]These eight rights are the subject of incessant work by Consumers International and consumer groups around the world, see:

It underwent a gradual enlargement, which certainly should not be treated as a complete and final process. It has somewhat been modified doctrinally as a result of which they developed the following directory:

J. the right to safety, protection of life and health,
K. the right to information and education,
L. the right to protection of economic interests,
M. the right to access to effective redress system,
N. the right to association, to be heard and represented.

Looking for the most comprehensive catalogue, one can reach for the position of consumers international in the opinion of which, the contemporary status of the consumer shall be appointed by the following right:

- The right to satisfaction of basic needs,
- The right to safety,
- The right to be informed,
- The right to choose,
- The right to be heard,
- The right to redress,
- The right to consumer education,
- The right to a healthy environment [67].

II. Definition of consumers rights:

Consumer rights are defined as:

https://www.opc.gouv.qc.ca/zone-enseignants/liste-activites/activite/droits-responsabilites-consommateur/#:~:text=Droit%20%C3%A0%20la%20satisfaction%20des,Droit%20%C3%A0%20un%20environnement%20sain
Accessed 25/08/2024.

[67] Wacinkiewicz, Ewelina Cała, op cit, pp20-22.

1- The right to satisfaction of basic needs:

Have access to basic essential goods and services: adequate food, clothing, housing, health care, education, utilities, water and hygiene [68].

The right to satisfaction translates today into the right to be treated well which allows the consumer to be treated fairly, respectfully and without discrimination by the company without taking into account the origins, status or opinions of consumers [69].

The right to satisfy basic needs also requires the right to equality by prohibiting the supplier of goods and services to discriminate unfairly against a person or category of persons in relation to access, priority, supply and pricing, and even in relation to the enforcement of judgment or termination of an agreement[70].

2- The right to safety:

Be protected against products, manufacturing processes and services that threaten health or life [71].

Many standards imposed on manufacturers aim to protect consumer safety. This right requires that companies place tested products on the market that comply with these standards. This includes physical security, but also protection against risks:

Chemical: harmful substances when inhaled, swallowed or in contact with skin

Electrical: anything that causes shock, fire or burns

Mechanical: everything that leads to injuries and accidents

---

[68] See; http://www.reajc.be/fr/spip.php?article42
Accessed 26/08/2024.

[69] Emma Ménébrode, "Consumer Rights", see;
https://lemagdelaconso.ouest-france.fr/dossier-819-droits--consommateur-trucs-astuces-essentiels-connaitre.html
Accessed 25/08/2024.

[70] W Jacobs, P Stoop, R van Niekerk, "Fundamental Consumer Rights Under the Consumer Protection Act 68 of 2008: a Critical Overview and Analysis", Vol 13 No 3, (2010). p 318.

[71] See; http://www.reajc.be/fr/spip.php?article42
Accessed 26/08/2024.

Digital: identity theft, threat to data security, malware…

Consumers must be warned of the risks associated with the use of a product and clear instructions for use must accompany it. When a defect is identified after being placed on the market, the company must immediately take corrective measures and recall the product or offer a repair solution[72].

3- The right to be informed:

The right to information is one of the most important for the consumers. It guarantees that the consumer has the essential data that will help them make the right choice before making a purchase. They must be reliable and complete on the product or service that interests the consumer, this information includes: Conditions of sale, Details of the characteristics of the product or service offered, The price, Warranty conditions, Risks (for health, safety or the environment), Delivery conditions (prices, deadlines, etc.), when it comes to online or distance sales or when the good or service is not available on the day of payment, Return or exchange policy, Possible additional costs. This information must be clear and not misleading, the seller is obliged to respond honestly and transparently [73].

4- The right to choose:

Being able to make a choice from a series of products and services offered at competitive prices with the assurance of satisfactory quality [74].

Consumer's right to select any goods or services or suppliers in the market freely, without coercion or intimidation. A supplier may not group or bundle goods by requiring, as a condition of entering into an agreement, that the consumer must buy other goods or services from that supplier.

---

[72] Emma Ménébrode , https://lemagdelaconso.ouest-france.fr/dossier-819-droits--consommateur-trucs-astuces-essentiels-connaitre.
Accessed 25/08/2024.

[73] Ibid

[74] See; http://www.reajc.be/fr/spip.php?article42
Accessed 26/08/2024.

The right to choose also includes the consumer's right to return goods, This includes goods in terms of an agreement arising out of direct marketing, in a case in which the consumer rescinded the agreement during the cooling-off period (which may be returned at the consumer's risk and expense), and goods that the consumer did not have the opportunity to examine before delivery and then rejected delivery; a mixture of goods in a case in which the consumer refused delivery, as well as a case in which goods intended to satisfy a particular purpose were then found to be unsuitable for that particular purpose [75].

5- The right to be heard:

Have consumer interests represented in the design and execution of government policies and in the development of products and services[76].

The aim of consumer protection law is to create fair business practices in respect of advertising and selling. One of the most important business practices is to be truthful in advertising and selling. Creating fair business practices in this regard will ensure that real competition between suppliers is made possible, which in turn leads to lower prices and better products. It will also lead to greater trust by consumers and better relationships between consumers and suppliers in the supply of goods and services[77].

6- The right to redress:

The right to repair is ensured by the obligation of a legal guarantee. It allows the consumer to demand repair, replacement or refund of goods if they are defective, do not work as advertised or do not match the description provided by the seller. Companies are required to rectify the problem within a reasonable time and at no additional cost, during a legally determined period. This period depends on the type of product. The seller or manufacturer may also extend this duration of protection, free of charge or upon payment of an extended warranty. [78].

---

[75] W Jacobs, P Stoop, R van Niekerk, op cit, p322-327.
[76] See; http://www.reajc.be/fr/spip.php?article42
Accessed 26/08/2024.
[77] W Jacobs, P Stoop, R van Niekerk, op cit, p334.
[78] Emma Ménébrode, opcit ;

7- The right to consumer education:

Acquire the knowledge and skills necessary to be informed, to make choices of goods and services with confidence, while being aware of the fundamental rights and responsibilities of the consumer and how to act on them [79].

One of the aims of the Consumer Protection law is to protect consumers from unconscionable, unfair, unreasonable, unjust or improper trade practices and any deceptive, misleading, unfair or fraudulent conduct. This is done, inter alia, by regulating unconscionable conduct, false, misleading or deceptive representations, fraudulent schemes and offers, pyramid schemes, auctions, waivers, deferrals, substitution of goods, and over-selling and over-booking[80].

8- The right to a healthy environment:

Live and work in an environment that does not threaten the well-being of present and future generations [81].

What is particularly interesting is that the general category of consumer protection is subject to further fragmentation. There is more and more talk of protecting the rights of the consumers of the health, air, postal, telecommunications and energy services. Referring this process to the subjective development of human rights preformed years ago, from which consumers rights developed. One can prove that the latter are still in the stage of formation. Hence, the above outlined consumer rights directory should not be treated as complete. Certainly for the foreseeable future - with the development of national policies in this area - the strengthening of the status of consumer rights will follow, by expanding the catalogue of their rights[82].

---

https://lemagdelaconso.ouest-france.fr/dossier-819-droits--consommateur-trucs-astuces-essentiels-connaitre.html
Accessed 25/08/2024.

[79] See; http://www.reajc.be/fr/spip.php?article42
Accessed 26/08/2024.

[80] W Jacobs, P Stoop, R van Niekerk, op cit, p346.

[81] See; http://www.reajc.be/fr/spip.php?article42
Accessed 26/08/2024.

[82] Wacinkiewicz, Ewelina Cała, op cit, p22.

Chapter 2.

The role of competition law in promoting consumers rights

The development of competition law led to taking into account the protection of consumers' interests within its objectives and scope of application. This was evident through the competition law and policy efforts to establish actual competition in the market with the aim of improving the consumer welfare. In this context, improving consumers' living conditions has become one of the most important goals (**I**). Competition legislation despite the controversy that this modern concept has witnessed between the views of economists and jurists Competition legislation despite the controversy that this modern concept has witnessed between the views of economists and jurists, and The development of the concept of Consumer welfare in competition laws and policy (**II**).

I. The correlation between promoting consumers rights and the Goals of competition law

Competition law is closely linked to the protection of consumer rights, even though consumer protection legislation is the natural field for establishing and protecting consumers rights, alongside civil law and constitutions. The manifestation of this correlation is due to the fact that protecting and maintaining competition in the market makes it reflect positively on consumers' rights[83].

The more competition is real and free between competitors in the market, the more this is reflected in the consumer's contractual position. The consumer becomes more concerned by professionals, and the consumer has the freedom to choose away from the arbitrary and misleading practices that appear in monopolistic situations. Therefore, competition enhances the consumer's interests and rights as long as consumers are Target market group.

In US competition law, the consumer welfare standard remains a guiding principle arguably the guiding principle of competition law and policy, in his blast against prevailing US antitrust law 'a policy at war with itself' Robert Bork declared

[83] For more details see : Sami Benhamla, "Competition Law, A Study in Light of Algerian Legislation According to the Latest Amendments and Comparison to Modern Competition Legislation", Numidia for printing, publishing and distribution, Constantine, (2016), pp22-23.

that 'the only legitimate goal of antitrust is the maximization of consumer welfare'. However, by what he beguilingly called 'consumer welfare' he appears to have meant the com- bined interests of consumers and producers[84].

In EU competition law, Administrative procedures on possible infringements of competition law need to be guided by the public interests that EU competition law pursues. That the European Commission's decisions ought to uphold the public interests protected by EU law is a general requirement of the rule of law, which underpins the EU legal system (Art. 2 TEU)[85].

The protection of consumers' economic interests is a public interest inherent in the goals of EU competition law enforcement. The ultimate public interest underlying competition law enforcement is the protection of the competitive process. This is also the case in EU competition law. Nevertheless, EU competition law also guarantees that consumers get a fair share of the economic benefits resulting from the effective working of markets[86].

For competition law and policy, consumer welfare is not the whole story, but it should be, and now is central to it. If, as I have tried to argue, attacks on the consumer welfare standard are not compelling, then it should not be dislodged. Major questions nonetheless remain, not just about the competition law treatment of particular types of conduct, but also about how the concepts of competition and consumer welfare relate to each other. The latter view, which I favour, involves consumer welfare in the notion of competition itself[87].

For that some writers[88], examined the topic of protecting consumer interests from the perspective of competition law in light of the expansion and multiplicity of its goals. Protecting consumer interests has become among the goals of modern competition law despite the presence of other priority goals such as protecting freedom of competition

---

[84] John Vickers, "Competition policy and the consumer welfare standard", Journal of Antitrust Enforcement, Published by Oxford University Press, (2024), pp1-3. See:
https://doi.org/10.1093/jaenfo/jnae038
Accessed 28/08/2024.

[85] Cseres, K. J., & Mendes, J. "Consumers' access to EU competition law procedures: outer and inner limits". Common Market Law Review, 51(2), (2014), p 489. See;
http://www.kluwerlawonline.com/abstract.php?area=Journals&id=COLA2014035
Accessed 28/08/2024.

[86] Cseres, K. J., & Mendes, J. op cit, p 484.

[87] John Vickers, op cits, p 11.

[88] Valérie Giacobbo Peyronnel," Consumer Protection through Competition Law: Jurisprudential Review", European Review of Competition Law, n3-4, (2010): p465.

in the market. Where the state intervenes in order to ensure the proper functioning of the market and preserve various interests, especially the private interests of consumers, and this is what led to the emergence of the general, protective and directive economic system, so that the consumer group is considered the primary beneficiaries of the competition law, which complements the consumer protection law[89].

Whatever, The Competition after all the primary form of competition that law and policy aim to protect. In these terms, competition is not only good for consumers, but competition-to-offer-consumers-good-deals is the competition that matters[90]. It follows that consumers' economic well-being is one of the core public interests pursued in the enforcement of competition law, irrespective of whether competition is considered as a means to achieve an end or as an end in itself[91].

II. The Development of Consumer welfare in competition laws and policy

The United Nations Economic and Social Commission for Western Asia (ESCWA) has defined consumer welfare as the individual benefits derived from the consumption of goods and services.

In theory, individual welfare is defined by an individual's own assessment of his/her satisfaction, given prices and income. Exact measurement of consumer welfare therefore requires information about individual preferences92.

The concept of improving consumer's well-being has witnessed legislative and judicial development in Europe, where the European judiciary adopted the concept of improving consumer's well-being in the European Court's decision issued on June 7, 2006. This contradicts the concept of protecting consumer interests, which addressed by the European judiciary in its decision issued on June 16, 1980 [93].

Therefore, this concept was promoted, which takes into account the benefits of consumers, which also appear in collective benefits, and which has become part of the

---

[89] Dominique Legais, Commercial and Business Law, (Paris, 22nd, Sirey, 2015), 358-360.

[90] John Vickers, op cits., p 8.

[91] Cseres, K. J., & Mendes, J. àp cit, p 491.

[92] Glossary of Industrial Organisation Economics and Competition Law, compiled by R. S. Khemani and D. M. Shapiro, OECD, (1993), see;
https://www.unescwa.org/sd-glossary/consumer-welfare
Accessed 08/09/2024.

[93] Valérie (B.P) .op. cit.pp 468 -483.

components of the economic system, considering that it requires ensuring that consumers benefit from low prices, freedom of choice between suppliers, a plurality of products and services, accessibility to them, and a guarantee of compensation, in the event of damage. On the other hand, the non-economic benefits of consumers are outside this framework, and this is what the European judiciary stated in its decision issued on February 19, 2002. So that the consumer remains the ultimate beneficiary of competition policy and that protecting his benefits intersects with the objectives of competition law, which is considered part of the economic system[94].

The concept of consumer welfare itself is not clearly defined; it is understood through the lens of economic efficiency calculations. Economists (and lawyers following their lead) calculate the losses and gains to consumer welfare of allowing a specific agreement between undertakings. Under what we will call a narrow consumer welfare approach, as primarily advocated by the European Commission, agreements between undertakings leading to an increase in price, a limitation in output (quantity, quality or range) or a limitation of innovation, are prohibited because they are considered detrimental to consumer welfare[95].

Economists call that 'total welfare' and reserve 'consumer welfare' for the interests of consumers leaving aside the profits of producers. I will therefore translate Bork as saying that 'the only legitimate goal of antitrust is the maximization of total welfare, The wider point is that competition law is about which rules to adopt, not which commercial decisions to take. Though perhaps not a clinching point, this weighs against total welfare and in favour of consumer welfare as the better economic standard for competition policy[96].

On the other hand, there are many statements suggesting that, from the European Commission's point of view, modern EU competition policy is largely about protecting consumer welfare.

Vice-President Almunia said in a speech shortly after he was nominated commissioner in charge of competition policy that of us here today know very well what our ultimate objective is: Competition policy is a tool at the service of consumers. Consumer welfare is at the heart of our policy and its achievement drives our priorities and guides our decisions. Consumers are mentioned in the article 101, it is stated that the prohibition under article 101is not applicable to agreements etc... Which contribute

[94] Valérie (B.P) .op. cit.pp 468 -483.

[95] Rutger Claassen & Anna Gerbrandy, op cit, p 3.

[96] John Vickers, op cit, pp 1-3.

to 'improving the production or distribution of goods or to promoting technical or economic progress, while allowing consumers a fair share of the resulting benefit'[97].

However, which public interest guides the enforcement of EU competition law is subject to debate. The Court of Justice has clearly stated that this public interest is "competition as such", stressing that EU competition rules aim to protect "not only the interests of competitors or of consumers, but also the structure of the market" (our emphasis). This contradicts an earlier judgment of the General Court, where that Court, stressing the relevance of consumer welfare as part of the objectives of competition law, considered the well-being of consumers as the "ultimate purpose" of competition law. The positions of the two Courts indicate different ways of interpreting how the overall material welfare of society, which competition law generally aims to increase by maintaining rivalry among firms, relates to the protection of consumer interests. In general, the final objective of competition policies can either be considered to be the protection of the competitive process as such, to which the interests of consumers are subordinated, or the immediate (and short-term) interests of consumers[98].

Some also considered that the appreciation of 'well-being' and 'welfare' might not have identical meanings, but this surely indicates that the consumer welfare standard is centrally important for understanding the law on abuse of dominance. It is also made plain that consumer benefits go way beyond price[99].

The currently dominant approach in European competition law is the consumer welfare approach, especially since the Commission advocates it. This approach focuses on the outcomes of market exchanges, and does so by considering their effects on (aggregate) consumer welfare[100].

Accordingly, protecting consumers welfare has become one of the most prominent goals of modern competition legislation, which leads to enhancing their rights, especially with regard to freedom of choice and the alternatives that the

---

[97]Svend Albæk, "Consumer Welfare in EU Competition Policy", Economics, Law, Political Science, (2013), p 68. See
https://competition-policy.ec.europa.eu/system/files/2021-09/consumer_welfare_2013_en.pdf Accessed 02/09/2024.

[98] Cseres, K. J., & Mendes, J, op cit, p 489.

[99] John Vickers, op cits, p 6.

[100] Rutger Claassen & Anna Gerbrandy," Rethinking European Competition Law: From a Consumer Welfare to a Capability Approach", Volume 12, Issue 1 (January 2016), p2.
http://doi.org/10.18352/ulr.321

consumer finds when there are multiple players in the market and when there is real competition in it.

Section 3.

Protective aspects of consumers rights

The protective aspects of consumer rights include contractual protection for consumers within the framework of their contractual relations against evaders in the market who enjoy a better contractual position than consumers because of the cognitive and technical superiority they enjoy. Therefore, the legislator intervened to establish rights for consumers within the framework of contracting, especially distance contracting in which relevant data is used. The personal nature of consumers. Therefore, modern legislation has approved the protection of consumer privacy when implementing digital contracts.

Consumer protection associations also constitute a mechanism to protect and defend consumer rights, especially at the judicial level, as recent legislation has approved consumer protection associations' ability to file collective lawsuits to protect consumer interests.

Chapter 1.
Promoting consumer rights in contractual relationships

It is one of the most important consumers rights that requires attention. Which those related to concluding and execution contractual relations, whether in face to face or from a distance, as strengthening these rights leads to strengthening the contractual protection of consumers in consumption contracts?

Therefore, the civil code and consumer protection legislation focused on these rights, most of which constitute legal obligations imposed by the legislator on producers, distributors, and service providers in the market. This is what led to the establishment of a protective public order, since the consumer category constitutes a weak party in contractual relations, and this is what justified legislators' intervention to approve a set of contractual obligations for the benefit of consumers within the consumer protection legislation (I).

The importance of addressing consumer rights also increases when it comes to contractual relationships that take place remotely via digital and electronic supports, and this is especially evident in the consumer's right to withdraw as long as he has not seen the seller in a sensory vision. In this context, Islamic law takes precedence in importance interest to the rights of consumers when contracting, as it is also credited with establishing many of these rights, especially the right to withdraw, in addition to the rights related to protecting consumer satisfaction, such as the right to information, or protecting the product, such as guaranteeing defects, etc **(II).**

I. Reasons for legal protection of consumers rights in contractual relationships

The concept of contractual protection for the consumer changed with the emergence of consumer protection legislation in light of the shortcomings known in the contractual provisions in the civil code, and this led to the expansion of the scope of contractual protection for the consumer.

The principle of the authority of will has remained a safety valve for contractual relations and a solid foundation for contractual freedom, as the contract constitutes the law of the contracting parties. Which gives many positive guarantees to the contracting parties at the stage of contract formation. The principle of contractual freedom has remained dominant in the contractual field despite attempts to limit its consequences in light of recent economic, social and industrial developments that have proven the deficiency of the principle of the power of will in achieving contractual balance and contractual justice between contracting parties[101].

The reason is that if the two parties reach an agreement, the basis of this agreement is the contract law, meaning that the law is the one that implements their agreement. Therefore, there was no paternalistic intervention by the courts on the basis that the agreement or condition appeared unreasonable in an earlier era in which contracts were negotiated and the parties were in an equal negotiating position. However, this absolute principle has been curtailed by common law, which will not enforce a contract if it is contrary to public order[102].

The civil code, in its conception of the provisions of the general theory of the contract, is based on the presumed equality between the contracting parties. What matters is abstract equality, as if each of the contracting parties has the same rights and the same duties. As for consumption legislation, it seeks to achieve equality, given that the hypothesis on which it is based is inequality, knowing that the disparity what exists between the consumer and the intervener is of a social and economic nature. Therefore, the Consumer Protection Law enshrined new principles, such as the obligation to inform, conformity, and others, which may in the future replace the general theory of the contract. This is because the main reason for the existence of consumer legislation is to protect the consumer, as he is a socially and economically weak party. Despite the fact that the consumer enjoys full capacity and the same rights as Enjoyed by the intervener, his social and economic situation prevents him from being able to uphold his rights, especially against abusive clauses[103].

In order to establish contractual protection for the consumer as a weak party, the European legislator tried to strengthen contractual protection for the consumer under European Directive No. 204-83, as well as the French legislator, who introduced several successive fundamental amendments to the consumer law in 2014, 2015 and

---

[101] Sarah Bellamy, "The Scope of Freedom of Contract in the Light of the Development of Contract Law," Journal of Research in Contracts and Business Law, Université Mentouri Constantine 1, A.S. for Printing and Advertising, Constantine, Volume 03, No. 5, (2018), pp. 105 et seq.

[102] W Jacobs, P Stoop, R van Niekerk, op cit, p 353.

[103] Ali Filali, "Contractual Freedom: An Old Concept and a Renewed Reality," Journal of Research in Contracts and Business Law, University of the Mentouri Constantine 1, A.S. for Printing and Advertising, Constantine, Volume 03, No. 5, (2018), pp. 24 et seq.

2016 with the aim of activating the protection established for the consumer. In consumption contracts, especially in distance contracting, As well as protecting it against abusive clauses and strengthening the obligation to inform before contracting, as these provisions came to take into account the position of the contracting parties, in contrast to the rules of civil code (the general theory of contract), which do not recognize the existence of a difference between the contracting parties, so that the profession or economic status of the contracting party is not taken into account[104] .

With the aim of protecting consumer satisfaction, the French legislator, within the framework of the amendments it brought, strengthened consumer protection before contracting by establishing the obligation to inform before contracting, regardless of the nature of the contract, and this is in addition to the general obligation to inform. It also strengthened the consumer's right to withdraw from distance contracts, whether by phone, electronically, or at home. It also approved the prohibition of forced sales and all unfair and aggressive practices, and strengthened oversight mechanisms and the powers of oversight agents and administrative authorities in the field. Investigation and imposition of administrative fines without the need to notify the judiciary, with increased criminal penalties[105].

The economic public order appeared clearly and independently with the beginning of the intervening state, which was preoccupied with the economic field. Its most important principles are freedom of trade and industry and freedom of competition. As for the protectionist public order, its provisions aim to protect economically and socially weak groups in the face of others who are in an economic, social, or cognitive position better. It imposes its conditions on the various legal relationships that exist between them, such as the disparity that exists between producers and consumers, which prevents the weak party (the consumer) from being able to adhere to his contractual freedom. Therefore, the provisions of social public order aim to reduce this disparity by providing protection for these vulnerable groups, such as the consumer's acknowledgment of the right to guarantee the product from all defects. His right to seek recourse against anyone intervening in the process of marketing the product, and obligating the producer to notify the consumer of information about the product, how to use it, its characteristics, and its components.

---

[104] Jacques Chestin," Treatise on Civil Law, Consumer Contracts: Common Rules", LGDJ, Paris, (2011), 11 -13.

[105] Chloé Minet , op .cit :44 - 49 .

Any agreement contrary to this shall be void and shall be replaced by the provision of law established for such law[106].

In this context, consumer law is considered a social market law because it aims to ensure consumer protection, and it is considered a fundamental law[107].

Therefore, protecting the interests of consumers has become part of the foundations of the general protective economic order, the provisions of which aim to protect the weak contractor from the abuses of the other contractor within the framework of contractual relations[108].

Consumer law has taken a collective approach thanks to the development witnessed by the concept of the public interest, which also includes the interest of consumers. This is what led to the emergence of a new public order called the social or protective public order that protects the weak party109.

This new approach that distinguishes consumer law comes from the fact that this law combines various fields. It is not considered a class law, but rather a private law that is complementary at the same time to the civil law (common law). Therefore, it is not considered an independent law, because it does not protect the interests of the consumer in isolation, while the issue of reality and the codification of consumer law remains a subject of controversy and continuous development[110].

II. The interesting to the rights of consumers contracting in Islamic law

The idea of the interesting to the rights of consumers within the contractual relations was not the result of modern legislation. Islamic law was the first to do so, as these dates back to the beginning of the seventh century AD. Then, the interest of Islamic jurisprudence in protecting the contractor within the contractual relationship emerged through the detailed provisions it brought. Islamic jurisprudence, mainly related to the jurisprudence of sales **(1).**

---

[106] Ali Filali, "Introduction to Law", Movem Publishing, Algeria, (2010), pp. 147-148.
[107] Nicolas Mathey, op cit, p 1.
[108] Ali Filali, Obligations: The General Theory of Contract, Movem Publishing, Algeria, (2012), pp. 280 et seq.
[109] Ali Filali, "Consumer Law: An Adaptation of Common Contract Law ", Review the Annals of the University of Algiers 1, vol 2, n° 27 (2015): 38.
[110] Nicolas Mathey, op cit, p2.

Islamic jurisprudence also established some modern aspects of protection for the consumer, and this is evident in remote contractual relations, where the vision option theory emerges as a mechanism to protect the contractor in electronic and digital contracting **(2).**

1- **Establishing Islamic law for consumer rights related to contractual consumer protection**

Islamic Sharia jurists paid attention to the contractual protection of the consumer, even though the concept of the consumer did not appear explicitly within the provisions of financial transactions among Islamic Sharia jurists, given that the concept of the contracting party in general, and the concept of the buyer in particular include the concept of the consumer, which is considered a modern concept recently approved by consumer protection legislation. This is also the case with the concept of consumers rights[111].

This interest was evident in many of the legal provisions that dealt with the jurisprudence of sales, and this is what appears in the provisions related to protecting the consent of the contracting party in contracts, whether related to the person and capacity of the contracting party[112], or protecting his consent from defects of will[113], in addition to the provisions related to the subject of the contract and its reason[114].

Due to the importance of these issues, Islamic Sharia jurists have established these controls that aim to establish and preserve the rights of consumers in the context of financial transactions and protect consumer satisfaction, especially from defects that

---

[111] Consumer rights can be defined as: those rights that represent a set of rules obligatory for the consumer that protect his economic interests and regulate his contract with the other party. See: Al-'Alī Ṣāliḥ aḥmyd, (In Arabic) "Ḥuqūq al-mustahlik fī al-fiqh al-Islāmī wa-al-qānūn : dirāsah muqāranah", Majallat Jāmi'at al-Shāriqah lil-'Ulūm al-shar'īyah wa-al-Dirāsāt al-Islāmīyah, Vol 17, n 2, Decemder,2020.p 753.

[112] It is required for the contracting party to discriminate. If he is not discriminating, he is not qualified to enter into any contract, otherwise the contract will be invalid. The failure to discriminate is either due to minors, insanity, or imbecility. See:
Al-Ṣaghīr 'Abd al-'Azīz ibn Muḥammad, (In Arabic) al-mu'āmalāt fī al-sharī'ah al-Islāmīyah, al-Markaz al-Qawmī lil-Iṣdārāt al-qānūnīyah, Cairo, 2016, pp75-89.

[113] The defects of the will are: error, deception, coercion, and fraud.

[114] When the subject of the contract is in violation of the rulings of Sharia, such as selling forbidden things, or a contract is invalidated due to the failure of one of its descriptions due to ignorance, or the failure of witnesses, etc. See Al-Ṣaghīr 'Abd al-'Azīz ibn Muḥammad, Ibid, pp90-91.

may appear in the merchandise. Therefore, Islamic Sharia jurists have approved the prohibition of corrupt sales[115].

One of the manifestations of Islamic jurisprudence's interest in the contractual rights of consumers is the provisions related to the prohibition of food fraud, deception, and all forms of deception in the field of contracting, which are considered among the most important provisions that came to prohibit these practices that affect consumer rights because they cause severe harm to the economic interests of consumers.

It was stated in **Al-Muwatta'** that **the Prophet, may God's prayers and peace be upon him**, forbade the sale of ambiguity, which is something that has an apparent appearance that tempts the buyer and an unknown hidden meaning, which is a risk[116].

Any contract of sale, lease, or rental with risk or deception regarding a price, value, or term is not permissible. It is not permissible to sell deceit, nor is it permissible to sell something unknown or for an unknown term. fraud or deception is not permissible in sales Neither picturesque nor deceitful, neither deception nor concealment of faults, mix bad with good, or conceal anything about his merchandise if the buyer dislikes it or mentions it because it is cheaper for him in the price[117].

2- **The option of visibility as a manifestation of consumer rights protection in distance contracting**

The topic of consumer protection in distance contracting was not known in modern legislation until after the emergence of electronic contracting and digital contracting in which the consumer does not see the product with a physical vision, where consumer protection legislation recognized the consumer's right to withdraw, and despite the fact that distance contracting was not known to jurists Islamic Sharia. However, Islamic Sharia addressed the issue of consumer protection in distance contracting Which was known to ancient Islamic Sharia jurists as a contract between absent parties, so that the contractor who did not see the item was given the option of seeing it, which enables him to withdraw from the contract. The latter gives the contractor the authority to sign or annul the contract, as is the case in electronic

115 Ibn Juzay' Abū al-Qāsim, (In Arabic) al-qawānīn al-fiqhīyah, Dār al-Fikr, Beirut, 2009, p220.
116 Al-Suyūṭī 'Abd al-Raḥmān, (In Arabic) Is'āf almubbṭ' bi-rijāl almūṭ', Ṭ 5, Manshūrāt Dār al-Āfāq al-Jadīdah, al-Maghrib, 1999, p578.
117 Al-Ābī Ṣāliḥ ibn 'Abd al-Samī' A, (In Arabic) al-Thamar al-Dānī 'alá Risālat al-Qayrawānī, Dār al-Faḍīlah, Cairo, 2010.pp529-530.

commerce contracts today. This constitutes an enhancement of consumer rights within the distance contracting[118].

The importance and status of the vision option is evident in the field of sales in order to protect the consent of the weak contractor, especially in the field of electronic commerce, which is considered the ideal environment for distance contracting, where consent is considered one of the pillars of the sale. It is not valid to sell without the consent of both parties, according to his saying, **may God's prayers and peace be upon him: "The Selling is based on satisfaction**"[119] .

In order to enhance the freedom of the contractor and protect his consent in contracting remotely, Islamic law recognized the right of choice for the contractor as a guarantee to protect his consent and knowledge of the action he is undertaking as well as the subject of the contract.

Jurisprudential interpretations of the sighting option varied among Islamic Sharia jurists. Some of them based the sighting option in view of the considerations that are based on protecting the consent of the contracting party. Some of them attributed it to the necessity of describing the product to the contractor as long as that is considered one of the components of the contract. Some of them attributed it to the necessity of the contractor seeing the product in order to Contract running out. In this context, the sighting option relates to the protection of the contractor who did not see the product at the contract council, so approving this option for him amounts to contractual protection when he sees the product.

There is no doubt that the vision option was legislated for the buyer to take his time to think and advice. The same basis on which the right of withdrawal is based, which relates to the satisfaction of the consumer, who benefits from an additional

---

[118] The contracting party's options are divided into two parts: some of them are proven by the text of Sharia even if one of the contracting parties does not stipulate them, including the visibility option and the option of defect, and some of them are proven by agreement of the contracting parties, such as the option of condition and the option of designation. This is to achieve justice and prevent injustice in transactions and achieve complete satisfaction and expansion for the contracting parties and taking care of their interests.
For more details, see: Zaydān 'Abd al-Karīm, (In Arabic) Al-Madkhal li-Dirāsat al-sharī'ah al-Islāmīyah, Mu'assasat al-Risālah, Beirut, 1996, p 314.

[119] It was narrated by Ibn Majah on the authority of Abu Saeed Al-Khudri, with a chain of transmission traceable to the Prophet, in Al-Tijarat, Chapter on Selling Options, Hadith No. 2185, and the investigator Muhammad Fuad Abd al-Baqi said: Its chain of transmission is authentic and its narrators are trustworthy.
See Al-Sin, Dar Revival of Arabic Books, Cairo, Egypt, without year and edition number: 737/2

period of thought subsequent to that is subsequent to the contract[120]. Which allows him to think carefully about the suitability of the product to his legitimate desires.

Thus, Islamic law is the material source that established the principles and provisions upon which it is based Consumer rights in contractual relationships, especially those developed in the digital space and e-commerce, which have been recently included in consumer protection legislation, whether before contracting, at the conclusion of the contract, or at its execution.

[120] Ali Filali, Muhammad Imad al-Din Ayyad, "Obligations, General Theory of Contract and Obligation by Unilateral will", 4th edition, National Office for Educational Works and Training, Algeria, (2023), pp 458-460.

Chapter 2.

Establishing consumer rights in the digital space When processing data of a personal nature

With the vogue of e-commerce, the expansion of digital contracting, and the dominance of the American digital economy giants (GAFAMs) despite China's competition. Taobao, Jindong, Weihaodian, Amazon and other platforms have become an inseparable part of many consumers' daily lives[121].

The digital revolution opened several unprecedented horizons for economic actors as well as consumers, as digitization led to a reconsideration of traditional economic models as well as existing power relationships in the market between various actors, especially after the emergence of digital markets and digital intermediaries as platforms that work to bring the largest possible number of Consumers [122].

Therefore, consumer data of a personal nature has become a subject of interest for jurists, considering that this affects the privacy of the individual. For this reason, modern legislation flattered to protect data of a personal nature has approved a set of rights that the consumer enjoys in the context of the use and processing of his data of a personal nature by authorities concerned or companies that work to collect and use these data.

These rights appear in: the right to information, access to data, and the right to retrieve it **(I).** As well as the right to restrict and object to the processing of personal data and to correct or delete it **(II).**

---

[121] Alina Quach , ibid
https://www.lagbd.org/Produire_et_distribuer_en_Chine_:_le_renforcement_de_la_protection_des_consommateurs_(cn)#II._La_nouvelle_loi_de_protection_des_droit_des_consommateurs_du_25_octobre_2012_.28en_vigueur_le_15_mars_2014.29
accessed 24/8/2024

[122] Nicolas Petit and Pieter Van Cleynenbreugel, European Competition Law and the Digital Economy, The Hague, FIDE XXXIX Congress the Hague (2020) p 1.

I. The consumer's right to be informed of the processing, access and retrieval of his personal data

The right of the consumer to be informed about the processing of his data of a personal nature (1) and to access (2) and retrieve it (3), represents one of the most important consumer rights in the digital space.

1. The consumer's right to be informed of the processing of his personal data

Among the basic rights that the consumer enjoys in the context of the processing of his personal data is his right to prior notification by the processing responsible, as the latter is required to inform the consumer explicitly and unambiguously about the issue of collecting and using his personal data. With the reason of the purpose of the processing, the nature of the data subject to processing, its objectives and details related to it. The processing responsible is also required to inform consumers of the details related to his identity, as well as the purpose of the processing and every useful piece of information, especially if the processing results in the transfer of his rights to a foreign country.

Otherwise, excludes from the scope of the obligation of information, the issue of processing data of a personal nature whose purpose is to carry out statistical or historical operations or related to scientific research issues[123].

2. The consumer's right to access data of a personal nature

Access allows each interested person to go to the institution responsible for processing personal data in order to find out whether his or her personal data is being processed, so that he or she can obtain information related to the data and communicate with the concerned institution.

Whatever, the person responsible for the processing is required to state the reason and purpose of the processing, as well as to state the category of personal data concerned with the processing and the party or institution concerned with the data, especially if the topic relates to a country or an international organization, in addition

---

[123] Right of access to personal data, electronic documentation, Dalloz, (June 2021).

to the guarantees granted to the consumer in the event that personal data is transferred to Another institution.

The processing responsible must also inform the consumer of his right to be informed of the right of access, as well as the information that must be provided before or after collecting the information, unless the processing is related to state security or defence, and exercising the right of access is subject to some restrictions,

The processing responsible can reject the access request when the request is unfounded or exaggerated, as is the case if the request is repeated several times, or if the request violates rights and freedoms when it comes to sensitive information, or if the topic is related to violating the private lives and data of people, or when it is related to Addressing the issues and requirements of scientific or historical research[124].

3. The consumer's right to retrieve his personal data

This right allows the concerned person to retrieve data of a personal nature that was provided to the company or to the electronic supplier that transferred it to others or kept it for a personal purpose. This right constitutes a protective mechanism, but it does not lead to its deletion.

This requires the consent of the person concerned and that he be one of the parties to the contract in order to exercise this right, which allows him to retrieve data of a personal nature as well as knowing whether this data has been transferred to another processing institution.

Whatever it is, the right to retrieve data remains independent of and different from the right to delete, in that the right to retrieve does not lead to deleting data, but rather to sharing it, not transferring it[125].

The data is retrieved either by downloading it into the data subject's account, and the processing responsible transfers the data after the data subject accepts it in a clear and legible manner and informs the data owner of it.

The processing responsible may also reject the request when retrieving data would prejudice the rights and freedoms of others, or when the topic relates to

[124] Right of Access to Personal Data, Ibid.

[125] Right to Portability, Personal Data, electronic documentation, Dalloz, (February 2020).

processing necessary to carry out the tasks of a public service or public authority, or when the request is ill-founded and exaggerated, or when it relates to sensitive data[126].

II. The right to restrict and object to the processing of personal data and to correct or delete it

The right of the consumer to restrict **(1)** and object to the processing of his personal data **(2)** and to correct or delete **(3)** it represents one of the most important consumer rights that enhance his legal position in the digital space, and this is what we will try to explain in turn.

1. The right to restrict the processing of personal data

The consumer can submit a request to freeze the use of his personal data due to a special reason, as he can stop processing the data but without deleting it, in which case the concerned authority will refrain from processing his data.

However, the processing responsible still has the possibility of preserving it, especially in the event of a dispute over the data, or if the processing is illegal and the person concerned requests its deletion, or when the processing responsible does not use this data, but rather saves it only in order to prove, exercise, or defend rights before the judiciary.

In addition, when the processing responsible objects to the processing for reasons related to his or her own situation, then the processing can be frozen, the same applies in the event of a lawsuit[127].

Moreover, the processing of data cannot be frozen except in cases where the person concerned provides his consent or when there is a justified necessity for processing in view of the necessity of proving the exercise of defending rights before the judiciary or the necessity of protecting the rights of others or the existence of reasons related to the public interest. In this context, it is necessary to inform the person concerned about this, and the processing responsible can reject the freezing request in

---

[126] Ibid.

[127] Right to Limit the Processing of Personal Data, Electronic documentation, Dalloz, (June 2021).

the event that the request is not established or exaggerated, or in the event of a violation of rights and freedoms, or when it comes to sensitive data[128].

2. The right to object to the processing of personal data

The right to object allows every interested person to object to the processing of personal data that concerns him, especially if the topic is related to advertising or commercial purposes.

The processing responsible may reject the objection request when there are legitimate justifications based on the interests, rights and freedoms of the person concerned that justify the processing of the data in question, as is the case with data necessary to prove or exercise rights before the judiciary, or when the consumer approves the processing, or when the processing is necessary for the execution of a contract to which the consumer is party, or when the processing is necessary to comply with a legal obligation to which the processing responsible is subject, or when the processing is necessary to preserve the vital interests of the consumer or when there is a provision excluding the right to object.

If the objection is accepted, the processing responsible stops processing the data without deleting it. However, if the objection is rejected, he must justify his rejection and inform the consumer of the methods and deadlines for the appeal[129].

3. The right to correct or delete data of a personal nature

The consumer may request updating, correcting, erasing, or closing his personal data being processed if the processing violates the law. In this context, the processing responsible is committed to making the necessary corrections as soon as possible.

The consumer also has the right to request that the processing responsible deletes his personal data that concerns him, especially in the cases:

- If the data are no longer necessary for the processing or when the data subject withdraws his or her consent to the processing or there is no legal justification for the processing.

---

[128] Ibid.

[129] Right of Opposition, Electronic documentation, Dalloz, (2021).

- When the data subject exercises his right to object in the absence of any benefit in retaining the data subject to processing
- If the data of a personal nature is the subject of unlawful processing or if it is necessary to delete the data in order to comply with a legal obligation or the legislation of one of the countries.
- If the data was then collected within the framework of offering a service directed to children.

Moreover, the processing responsible may refuse to delete data when it comes to exercising the right to expression and information, as well as respecting a legal obligation established by law or agreement, or execution the tasks of a public service or public authority, or for reasons related to the public interest in the field of public health, or for reasons related to archival documentation and scientific research Historical, or when the goal of the processing is not achieved if it is deleted, or when it comes to proving rights before the judiciary.

In the event that this data is deleted, the processing responsible must prove this from a technical standpoint and notify the parties to whom this data was directed. If the data is the subject of public dissemination, he must notify the rest of the processing responsible[130].

---

[130] Right to Erasure, Electronic documentation, Dalloz, 2021.

Chapter 3.

The role of consumer protection associations in defending consumer rights

Consumer protection associations contributed a major role in defending consumer rights and striving to protect them thanks to the growing collective awareness among consumer groups of the necessity of coming together to defend their interests in the face of professionals in the market.

The consumer protection legislation framed the tasks and authorities of consumer protection associations (I), as well as recognizing their representation before the courts to defend the interests of consumers (II).

I. The awareness and sensitization role of consumers rights by consumer protection associations

The associational movement played an important role in protecting consumer rights, given that freedom of assembly is considered one of the basic freedoms, and this is what was embodied in the Consumer Protection Law, which addressed the issue of consumer protection associations, which are considered a tool for protecting consumers.

In addition to its preventive role of raising awareness, sensitizing, and informing the public about issues related to hygiene, security, product conformity, warranty, and price transparency, as well as judicial representation before the judiciary as an exception to the general rule in the field of litigation, this enhances the defence of consumer interests derived from the collective approach to consumer law[131].

The mission of consumer advocacy associations is to inform consumers, advise them and help them resolve disputes arising from consumer contracts. It can also act

[131] Ali Filali; op cit: 14.

preventively to find amicable solutions, as well as represent the private or collective interests of consumers before the judicial court[132].

They can also act preventively, for example to request the withdrawal of a dangerous product from the market or the removal of unfair clauses in contracts.

They can contact official bodies, such as the National Agency for Food, Environmental and Occupational Health Safety (ANSES), the Competition Authority or the Commission of unfair clauses. Approved associations are authorized to defend the collective interest of consumers in court, to bring group actions, and to seek compensation for damages suffered by consumers[133].

In EU law, consumers can bring complaints before the Commission and national competition authorities, and participate in the respective administrative procedure. In this role, they contribute to the public enforcement pursued by competition authorities; deterring undertakings from law infringements and making them comply with the law. Consumers may also bring damages claims before national courts, in which case they enforce competition rules in private litigation, seeking compensation for the harm suffered. In general, consumers' knowledge of the day-to- day functioning of markets, in particular those in mass-market consumer goods, make consumers and consumer organizations important information providers for competition authorities by way of bringing complaints and/or initiating damages actions before national courts[134].

In this context, the emergence of collective lawsuits constituted a new mechanism for protecting consumer rights thanks to the development witnessed by consumer protection associations, and this is what prompted consumer protection legislation recently to be recognized before the courts in order to defend consumer interests.

II. Collective lawsuits as a mechanism to protect consumer rights.

The traditional rule holds that every individual judicial procedure requires the presence of character and interest in order for the lawsuit to be accepted. However, the

[132] See; https://www.service-public.fr/particuliers/vosdroits/F1126
Accessed 02/09/2024.
[133] The Guide to consumer associations 2023 in France, See:
https://www.inconso.fr/sites/default/files/files/pdf/guide_associations_consommateurs_2023_4.pdf
Accessed 02/09/2024.
[134] Cseres, K. J., & Mendes, J. op cit, p 484.

question arises in the case where the interest is multiple and common, allowing for the establishment of a collective lawsuit that includes the interests of everyone, and this is what justifies a return to the collective tendency[135].

Therefore, the topic of consumer protection has become a collective issue, it is an obligation that falls on society, which works to enhance consumer protection, and this is considered a new approach[136].

In this context, the collective lawsuit is considered a mechanism that aims to achieve several goals: being a deterrent mechanism to punish the professional civilly because of the damage he caused to the customer, as well as compensating the consumer. In addition to being a mechanism to limit the actions of institutions in the future[137].

Moreover, accredited consumer protection associations after joining them and granting them an agency in order to repair the damage may file the collective lawsuit. Therefore, joining the group is sufficient to obtain compensation. On the other hand, the joined consumer cannot take unilateral action against the professional under whose responsibility the liability arose within the framework of collective lawsuit[138].

The development witnessed by legal life in light of the expansion of the movement to protect consumer rights and their concentration within the framework of consumer protection associations has been reflected in the recognition of their right to litigate before judicial authorities, as well as the right to repair. This is what has been embodied in modern legislation, such as the French legislator, which included the collective lawsuits under Law 2014-344 issued on March 17, 2014. Which jurisprudence considered as a revolution in the procedural as well as the social aspect, given that the collective lawsuit represents an effective mechanism for resolving the disputes of the group of consumers concerned and repairing the economic damage that results from anti-competitive practices as well as unfair commercial practices. So that consumer protection associations can intervene before civil judicial authorities to

---

[135] Christophe Verdure, Some Reflections on the Emergence of Mechanisms: Collective Action, European Review of Consumer Rights, n° 3, (2014): 429 - 430.

[136] Ali Filali; “Contractual Freedom: An Old Concept and a Renewed Reality”, p 8.

[137] Hervé Leborgne, "The Role of Institutions and Consumer Associations", Lamy Business Law Review, n°105, (Paris 2015):65.

[138] Matthieu Dary, Antoine du Chastel, "Group Action, First Assessment and Perspectives", Lamy Competition Review, No. 45, (2015): p119.

obtain compensation for the damage that befell the consumer due to professional breach of legal and contractual obligations[139].

As for the Arab countries, both Qatari and Algerian legislators were the first to recognize the collective lawsuit and consider it as a modern judicial mechanism to protect consumer rights and their material and moral interests, especially if a group of consumers is exposed to common harm by the same company. This is what was stipulated in Paragraph 5 of Article 4 of Law No. (8) of 2008 regarding consumer protection 8/2008: "Taking into account the provisions of Law No. (12) of 2004 regarding private associations and institutions, it is permissible to establish consumer protection associations that aim to: ...defending the interests of the consumer..."[140].

Thus, the Qatari legislator has kept up with modern legislation that recognizes the mechanism of collective lawsuits as a modern mechanism for defending consumers' rights before the judiciary, and this is considered a positive approach in Qatari legislation.

As for Algerian legislation, the Algerian legislator has recognized the right of consumer protection associations to litigate before judicial authorities and pleading lawsuits against any companies in the market who violates his legal obligations stipulated in Law 04-02 applicable to business practices, as stipulated in article 65, and this is mainly related to commercial practices unfair[141].

Whatever, the adoption of collective lawsuit as a collective mechanism for demanding compensation makes it an effective mechanism for protecting consumer rights.

Thus, collective lawsuit become an effective mechanism for protecting the rights of consumers against the companies in the market, especially when it comes to low-cost products and services in which the consumer refuses to resort to the judiciary due to the litigation expenses he incurs.

---

[139] Matthieu Dary, Antoine du Chastel, op cit :118.

[140] See: https://www.almeezan.qa/LawView.aspx?opt&LawID=2647&language=ar
Accessed 25/09/2024.

[141] Refer to Article 14 et seq. of Law Applicable to Commercial Practices No.: 04-02 dated 5 Jumada al-Awwal 1425, corresponding to June 23, 2004, amended and supplemented by Law No. 10-06 issued on August 15, 2010.

These lawsuits also contributed to spreading awareness among consumer groups and informing them of their rights before the judiciary. And a mechanism to force those involved in the market to limit actions and practices that harm consumers.

Bibliography

Book:

- Ali Filali, Introduction to Law, Movem Publishing, Algeria, 2010.
- Ali Filali, Muhammad Imad al-Din Ayyad, "Obligations, General Theory of Contract and Obligation by Unilateral will", 4th edition, National Office for Educational Works and Training, Algeria, 2023.
- Dominique Legais, Commercial and Business Law, Paris, 22nd, Sirey, 2015.
- Jacques Chestin," Treatise on Civil Law, Consumer Contracts: Common Rules", LGDJ, Paris, 2011.
- Lorraine Conway, Brexit: UK consumer protection law, Commons Library Briefing, 2021.
- Sami Benhamla, "Competition Law, A Study in Light of Algerian Legislation According to the Latest Amendments and Comparison to Modern Competition Legislation", Numidia for Printing, Publishing and Distribution, Constantine, 2016.

Romanized books:

- Al-Ābī Ṣāliḥ ibn 'Abd al-Samī' A, (In Arabic) al-Thamar al-Dānī 'alá Risālat al-Qayrawānī, Dār al-Faḍīlah, Cairo, 2010.
- Al-'Alī Ṣāliḥ aḥmyd, (In Arabic) "Ḥuqūq al-mustahlik fī al-fiqh al-Islāmī wa-al-qānūn: dirāsah muqāranah", Majallat Jāmi'at al-Shāriqah lil-'Ulūm al-shar'īyah wa-al-Dirāsāt al-Islāmīyah, Vol 17, n 2, Decemder,2020.
- Al-Ṣaghīr 'Abd al-'Azīz ibn Muḥammad, (In Arabic) al-mu'āmalāt fī al-sharī'ah al-Islāmīyah, al-Markaz al-Qawmī lil-Iṣdārāt al-qānūnīyah, Cairo, 2016.
- Al-Sin, Dar Revival of Arabic Books, Cairo, Egypt, without year and edition number: 737/2
- Al-Suyūṭī 'Abd al-Raḥmān, (In Arabic) Is'āf almubbṭ' bi-rijāl almūṭ', Ṭ 5, Manshūrāt Dār al-Āfāq al-Jadīdah, al-Maghrib, 1999.
- Ibn Juzay' Abū al-Qāsim, (In Arabic) al-qawānīn al-fiqhīyah, Dār al-Fikr, Beirut, 2009.
- Zaydān 'Abd al-Karīm, (In Arabic) Al-Madkhal li-Dirāsat al-sharī'ah al-Islāmīyah, Mu'assasat al-Risālah, Beirut, 1996.

Articles:

- Ali Filali, "Consumer Law: An Adaptation of Common Contract Law ", Review the Annals of the University of Algiers 1, vol 2, n° 27,2015.
- Ali Filali, "Contractual Freedom: An Old Concept and a Renewed Reality," Journal of Research in Contracts and Business Law, University of the Mentouri Constantine 1, A.S. for Printing and Advertising, Constantine, Volume 03, No. 5, 2018.
- Bryner Gary C, "Consumer protection in the United States: Birth and decline of the regulatory approach: French journal of public administration, N°56" ,1990.
- Chloé Minet, "Hamon Law; Is Better the Enemy of Good?" Lamy Business Law Review, n° 93, 2014.
- Christian Bolze, "Society, Consumption", Legal Encyclopedia, ,1996.
- Christophe Verdure, Some Reflections on the Emergence of Mechanisms: Collective Action, European Review of Consumer Rights, n° 3, 2014.
- Cseres, K. J., & Mendes, J."Consumers' access to EU competition law procedures: outer and inner limits". Common Market Law Review, 51(2), 2014.
- Deutch, Sinai. "Are Consumer Rights Human Rights?" Osgoode Hall Law Journal 32.3 1994.
- Giliker, P. The Consumer Rights Act 2015 - a bastion of European consumer rights? Legal Studies, publisher policies. 2017.
- Hervé Leborgne, "The Role of Institutions and Consumer Associations", Lamy Business Law Review, n°105, Paris, 2015.
- John Vickers, Competition policy and the consumer welfare standard, Journal of Antitrust Enforcement, Published by Oxford University Press, 2024.
- Mathieu Combe, "On the use of the Charters of Fundamental Rights in the Fight against unfair clauses in contracts", Lamy Business Law Review, n° 100, 2006.
- Matthieu Dary, Antoine du Chastel, "Group Action, First Assessment and Perspectives", Lamy Competition Review, No. 45, 2015.
- Muhammad Akbar Khan, The Origin and Development of Consumer Protection Laws, Journal of Asian and African Social Science and Humanities, Vol. 3, No. 3, 2017.
- Natacha Sauphanor - Brouilland, "The impact of the Macron Law on Contractual Consumer Law", Contract Review, March, 2016.

- Nicolas Mathey, "Should we Defend Consumer Law", Review Contracts Competition Consumption, 2016.
- Nicolas Petit and Pieter Van Cleynenbreugel, European Competition Law and the Digital Economy, The Hague, FIDE XXXIX Congress the Hague ,2020.
- Right of access to personal data, electronic documentation, Dalloz, 2021.
- Right of opposition, Electronic documentation, Dalloz, 2021.
- Right to Erasure, Electronic documentation, Dalloz, 2021.
- Right to Limit the Processing of Personal Data, Electronic documentation, Dalloz, June 2021.
- Right to Portability, Personal Data, electronic documentation, Dalloz, 2020.
- Rutger Claassen & Anna Gerbrandy, Rethinking European Competition Law: From a Consumer Welfare to a Capability Approach, Volume 12, Issue 1, January, 2016.
- Sabine Bernheim-Desvaux and Guy Raymond, "Crossed Perspectives on the Reform of the legislative part of the Consumer Code", Consumer Competition Contracts Review (August-September ,2016.
- Sami Benhamla, Legislative Attention in Consumers' Rights, a New Approach within Modern Legislations: Qatari and Algerian Legislations as Models, International Review of Law, Qatar University Press, vol 13, n01, 2024.
- Sarah Bellamy, "The Scope of Freedom of Contract in the Light of the Development of Contract Law," Journal of Research in Contracts and Business Law, Université Mentouri Constantine 1, A.S. for Printing and Advertising, Constantine, Volume 03, No. 5, 2018.
- Sudanto, Asrizal Saiin, Zaitun, Legal Protection of Consumer in the Human Right, Bilancia Vol. 16 No. 1, Januari-Juni ,2022.
- Svend Albæk, Consumer Welfare in EU Competition Policy, Economics, Law, Political Science, 2013.
- Valérie Giacobbo Peyronnel," Consumer Protection through Competition Law: Jurisprudential Review", European Review of Competition Law, n3-4, 2010.
- Vanessa Mak, Standards of Protection: In Search of the 'Average Consumer' of EU Law in the Proposal for a Consumer Rights Directive, TISCO, European Review of Private Law, No 04, juin2010.
- W Jacobs, P Stoop, R van Niekerk, Fundamental Consumer Right Under the Consumer Protection act 68 of 2008: Acritical Overview and Analysis, vol, 13 No 3. (2010).

- Wacinkiewicz, Ewelina Cała "Consumer's Rights as a Special Category of Human Rights," International Journal on Consumer Law and Practice: Vol. 1, Article 2. ,2013.

Reports:

- Alina Quach, Report of the November 19, 2014 meeting of the Paris-Beijing/China International Commission of the Paris Bar.
- Emma Ménébrode, "Consumer Rights", (2024).
- Glossary of Industrial Organisation Economics and Competition Law, compiled by R. S. Khemani and D. M. Shapiro, OECD, 1993.
- The Guide to consumer associations 2023 in France.
- These eight rights are the subject of incessant work by Consumers International and consumer groups around the world.
- Written by a member of ICLG's international panel of experts, Consumer Protection Laws and Regulations Italy 2024.

Constitutions and Legislations:

Constitutions:

- Algerian constitution of 2020.
- Egyptian Constitution of 2019,
- Mauritanian Constitution of 1991.
- Moroccan Constitution of 2011.
- Syrian Constitution
- Tunisian Constitution of 2014.

Legislations:

- Law No. 39 of 2014 related to consumer protection
- Law on Consumer Protection, **Qatar**, No. (8) of 2008 amended by Decree Law No. (14) of 2011, and Law No. (7) Of 2018.
- Law relating to general rules for consumer protection, **Algeria**, No.: 89-02 dated the first of Rajab in the year 1409 corresponding to February 7, 1989.
- Law defining the rules applicable to commercial practices Commercial Practices, **Algeria,** No. 04-02 of 5 Jumada al-Awwal 1425 corresponding to June 23, 2004, amended and supplemented by Law 10-06 issued on August 15, 2010.
- Law relating to consumer protection and suppression of fraud, **Algeria**, No.: 09-03 issued on Safar 29, 1430 AH, corresponding to February 25, 2009, amended by the Supplementary Finance Law 2015. And the law of 2018.

- Law Containing the Constitutional Amendment of 2020, **Algeria**, No. 82 issued on December 30, 2020.
- Directive 2011/83/EU of the European Parliament and of the Council of 25 October 2011 on consumer rights, amending Council Directive 93/13/EEC and Directive 1999/44/EC of the European Parliament and of the Council and repealing Council Directive 85/577/EEC and Directive 97/7/EC of the European Parliament and of the Council Text with EEA relevance.
- Law No. 2024-449 of May 21, 2024 aimed at securing and regulating the digital space.
- Law No. 2004-575 of June 21, 2004 for confidence in the digital economy.
- Law Applicable to Commercial Practices No.: 04-02 dated 5 Jumada al-Awwal 1425, corresponding to June 23, 2004, amended and supplemented by Law No. 10-06 issued on August 15, 2010.
- Consumer Rights Protection Law of the People's Republic of **China**.

www.ingramcontent.com/pod-product-compliance
Lightning Source LLC
LaVergne TN
LVHW022312200926
848481LV00004B/1303
9798892487368